Cyber scams.

How they affect ebay, paypal and you.

A visual guide to 25 of the biggest Internet scams.

James Elliott

First published in 2007

Text and design by James Elliott

Email: james@thebestscams.com
Website: www.thebestscams.com

This book is neither endorsed nor supported by ebay, Paypal or any other companies that are mentioned in this publication.

Whilst the Information contained in this site has been presented with all due care, the Author does not warrant or represent that the Information is free from errors or omission. Please check the web site of www.thebestscams.com for any updates.

ISBN 978-1-84753-628-0

INTRODUCTION

We all know what scams are and the damage they can cause. Unfortunately most of us believe that we can easily spot scams from a distance, therefore assuming that we have nothing to worry about.

But if scams are so easy to spot then the question must be asked - why do scammers persist? The answer is that there are millions of people who fall victim to these scams every year, and that makes it a very profitable business for scammers.

Most victims of these scams believed that they would never be deceived, so how did it happen? One of the main reasons is that victims don't know what to look out for; they simply didn't know what a scam looked like.

This book is an attempt to teach Internet users on how to spot, and avoid, scams.

Some of these scams seem so outrageous that the casual user may laugh out loud and claim 'that doesn't really happen' or 'I wouldn't fall for that'.

It does happen, and there are victims on a daily basis.

Scams occur anywhere there is money. Currently the biggest targets are Paypal, ebay and financial institutes.

Each of these 'targets' has their own security division that is constantly overwhelmed with the amount of fraud reported daily, so the best defence is to not get caught in the first place.

Nearly all of these scams work because of ignorance, inexperience or lack of knowledge. While this book cannot give you the experience to successfully defend your self against all the major online scams, it will give you the knowledge.

One final note – every email that I have used in this book is a REAL email that I have received. None of the examples have been edited or condensed in any way (unless specified otherwise).

*Please note that eBay, Paypal, Microsoft, Blizzard, World of Warcraft, itfacts and Alexa are all trademarks of their respective owners.

There are no screenshots of the eBay website although there are screenshots of emails that have illegally used the eBay logo.

TABLE OF CONTENTS

<u>FACTS</u>

Facts for the Year 2006

- US$437 million was lost to online scams
- US$49.3 billion was lost to identity fraud
- 1.2 million Americans (unknowingly) gave their information to criminals
- 2.4 million phishing* attempts per month; of this 14,411 were successful
- 5,259 phishing* web sites operating in August (fake web sites)
- 685,000 identity theft cases were reported to authorities
- 7.92 million phishing* emails were sent daily
- US$6,383 is the average that a person lost to identity fraud
- 4.7 billion pounds was lost by UK Internet users
- 6% of online orders were rejected by merchants because of fraud suspicions
- 4% of online orders were fraud

Facts overall

- 32% of corporate users in India have fallen victim to a phishing* email
- 4.55 million Americans have fallen for the Nigerian letter scheme
- 70% of users have been fooled by a phishing* email
- 59 hours is how long it takes to rectify online fraud

* 'Phishing' is a fraudulent attempt to gain financial details from a victim; it will be explained in more detail further in this book.

All statistics are from www.itfacts.biz

Don't be a statistic.

PART 1 – BASICS

Chapter 1 - Who am I?

I suppose the real question here is 'who am I to write about cyberscams?'

First a bit of background on myself - I am University educated in computers, have been on the Internet since 1996 and have used computers since 1986 when my brother and I were given a good old _Commodore 64._
My sons believe that I built Stonehenge to act as a computer but I'm not _that_ old!

One of my email addresses, that I have had for 8 years, receives over 250 spam emails a day; I have the latest in email filters but about 15 a day still manage to get through that. Via these emails I have read thousands of scams; some were horribly written but others were good, very good.
I receive about 3 phishing emails a day.

I also run a web site called 'www.thebestscams.com' which is the basis of this book. The web site can't be that bad as I have received a few 'interesting' emails.
Below is an example of just such an email I received recently -
_"you web site stupid as you are
i need accounts to sell my items as ebay not let us, ebay not let us have accounts so need
other account. i not anything wrong, if i did i be in jail as police not allow this - so you
are wrong, you web site wrong, you teach wrong, you one who should be in jail"_
I have also had conversations with the perpetrators of scams so it is an interesting web site to run.

Lastly, I am a victim of fraud.
In 2005 I was nearly eligible to become a powerseller on ebay, I only needed one more month of good sales to qualify.
Suddenly the invitation to become a powerseller arrived in my inbox to which I readily accepted; only to find out that the email wasn't real and I had just handed over my account details to professional criminals.
Luckily, for me, ebay have a professional anti-fraud division who shut down my account before any harm could be done.

Chapter 2 - Why they do it and who are they?

Scams are run for the same reason people rob banks – a quick financial gain.

In Australia the biggest scam I have heard of involved selling 200 iPods for $150 each (they usually sell for $400) over a weekend – this resulted in the criminals making $30,000 profit in 2 days (it was all profit as the iPods didn't exist).
To put that into perspective the average yearly wage in Australia is $26,000.

Fraud, via the Internet, is very easy and cheap to do, without exposing a criminal to any real risks. These criminals are very difficult to catch and even more difficult to prosecute.
African scammers bring in much needed foreign currency so their Government is not in any rush to shut them down.

So who are these people? There are many types of scammers but they have one thing in common – they don't consider what they are doing is wrong.
If you do get conned by these people you MUST admit, to yourself, that you have made a mistake; and then stop dealing with these people. There has NEVER been an instance of a scammer returning funds for any reason, don't waste your time trying; in fact there are several reasons not to try.
If you ask a scammer for your money back because you have cancer, for example, then the scammer will try to convince you to keep going; they will turn everything around because they are experienced in running scams.
The next sting they use on a victim may involve the scammer claiming that they themselves have cancer! Scammers learn from one scam to the next.

When I say 'stop dealing with these people' – I really do mean stop, don't send another email.
If you email them for any reason (even abusive) they believe that you are still 'in the game'; and to them it really is just a game.

Chapter 3 - Why the scammers targeted YOU!

You're special to your family and friends, but not to a scammer.

Scammers will use any means necessary to contact as many people as possible in the shortest amount of time; on the Internet this includes running programs that acquire your email address in order for them to send you the bait email.

Millions of emails are sent each day in the hope that one or two will be successful (I have seen figures that suggest that there are about eight 'successes' per one million sent).

If you really were special to them then the email wouldn't start with 'Dear friend ...' (or 'undisclosed recipients'), it would start with your name.

> **From:** rebecca20051960@hotmail.com **To:** undisclosed-recipients:,
> **Subject:** Order Inquiry

Also note the 'to' area of the email, it states that the email is being sent to 'undisclosed recipients'; email sent directly to you would show your email address.

So why is this email sent to 'Undisclosed-recipients'? Because it is a lot easier for scammers and their computer programs.

Remember that scammers must send millions of emails out each day in order to make a full time living. An American spammer (scams usually start from spam) was sent to prison for 9 years, during the case it was revealed he was sending up to 10 million emails per day.

For a scammer to send this many emails out they need to have a fast and efficient system, by sending to 'undisclosed-recipients' they can send out emails twenty to a hundred times faster.

The worst thing you can do with these emails is reply to them - **DON'T**.

Scammers don't know if you exist before they send their scam emails; if you reply then you have proved your existence and that is not what you want as they will send you thousands more.

Do not reply to them asking for them to stop sending these emails as again you have proved your existence. (You replied, therefore you are!)

Do not be tempted to reply to these emails with a smart arse comment or condemning what they do; they will either laugh you off or, if they are offended, hack your computer.

Scammers are usually professional hackers who can do a lot of damage to your computer, so don't be tempted to attack them; at the very least they can send you millions of emails (more commonly known as 'mail bombing') that will permanently crash your email system.

Don't think that you are the only one they are sending these spam emails to; one major spamming group was accused of sending out 100 million emails *per day*.

Getting your email address

So how do scammers get hold of your email address? It's actually very simple and there are three common methods.

The first method is to use a computer program that scans web pages for email addresses. If you write your email address in a forum board (for example) then their program will find it.
At the bottom of some pages on my web site I have written 'I can be contacted at james@thebestscams.com'; the scammers program will read the page and put my email address into their database.

The second method is even easier for a scammer - they simply get all the addresses from chain letters. Most people on the Internet send chain letters onwards which makes the scammers life a lot easier. The most common 'chain letters' are 'quizzes' that your friends send you.
Have you ever received a chain letter or a quiz? They ask you to send it on as quickly as possible; you probably do this without realising that all of the email addresses are being put into a spam database.

The screen shot below is an email that my son received (he uses my account); he did the quiz and then sent it on. I freaked when he told me that he had sent it on, I sat him down and explained why. Luckily he realised what he had done wrong; I also asked him to tell his friends not to send these sorts of 'quizzes' to us anymore.
In the screenshot you can see how many email addresses are visible, both in the 'To:' section and the body of the email. I have made lots of black marks on the screenshot to blot out any email addresses.

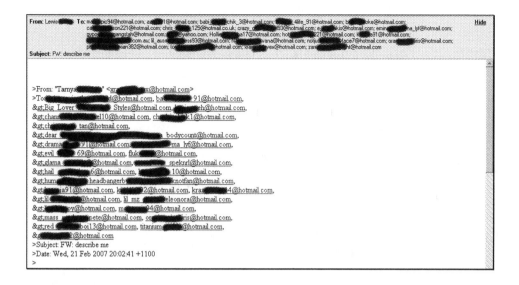

The third method is to sign you up to a newsletter; note that this was big several years ago but has since died.

Most web sites offer to send you a daily (or weekly) newsletter straight to your email address; all you had to do was supply your email address (naturally).

A lot of people would sign up for these. I know of a successful humour web site that has a subscriber list of 250,000 email addresses that they send a daily joke too.

Unfortunately most of these lists were either run by spammers or sold to spammers.

Chapter 4 - Tips when creating passwords

Some criminals don't even bother trying to trick you for your password – they simply guess it.

If a person knows your username they can then use computer software to try to guess your password. It tries to achieve this by using every word in the English language.
Some systems only allow a user to have three attempts at their password before it shuts the account down, but a lot of other systems don't; the criminals program can make over ten thousand guesses a second.

If your password is an English word then it WILL be hacked. It doesn't matter if it's a common word, a persons name or a medical term – it will be found out.

To circumvent this you need to make your password non legible; that could mean messing two letters up "mother = mohter" (okay), adding a number "mother = mother7" (good), jumbling up the numbers in the word "mother = mo1h3r" (great) or simply having a complete jumble of letters and numbers "hj34jui9" (best).

For more security you should consider changing your password on a regular basis. At university we were forced to change our passwords every 6 weeks for security reasons; considering we had access to the Microsoft Windows source code (which I never did get to see) then you can understand why security was so high.

Try not to use the same password on different web sites; if a low security web site is hacked and your password is stolen then it will be used on other web sites.
The perfect example of this is ebay and Paypal; if a fraudster gets your ebay password the first thing they will do is try it with your Paypal account – this account is usually linked to your credit card so it is quicker to loot than your ebay account (which is more enticing for the criminal).

Remember that having a person's ebay account is only the first step in scamming money and takes a lot of work, while having a paypal account is a simple case of looting the funds. It's the difference of robbing a bank of cash or robbing a warehouse of electronic goods in order to sell later - the bank is the easier option!

Chapter 5 - Why you will never be asked for your password

A database is simply a computer program that stores information. They can be simple (for example your DVD collection) or extremely complex (the entire US tax system). The largest, and most complex, databases in the world are insurance companies. Nearly every forum board on the Internet is a database.

These databases are crucial to the way these organizations work. For this reason they are very, very secure.

Normally there are only 2 ways of accessing this data.

The first way is how a person normally accesses this information – by using their username and password. If you use the wrong password then the database will not allow you access.

The second method of gaining access to a Database is for a person to have *'permissions'*. This is granted to staff members who are (usually) *'data administrators'*.

If you ring your bank (you were having problems with your account for example) you will speak to a person that has *'permission'* to view your bank details. They can view everything about your account (or any other customers).

While it may seem that staff with *'permissions'* have a lot of power they can't really do anything with it. The central computer logs everything they do; this is so management can review what they have done - including whose account they have viewed recently. If a staff member doesn't have a reason for viewing an account (having a look at a friends account because they were bored for example) then they will face disciplinary action.

So what's this got to do with people asking you for your password? It may seem legitimate that a staff member needs to ask you for your password in order to verify who you are.

Well, here's the trick – the staff member can see everything about your account *EXCEPT YOUR PASSWORD!* Trust me on this one; there is **NO COMMERCIAL DATABASE** in the world that displays passwords to the administrator.

So how can they verify whom you are if you don't supply your password? Easy, they can see your name, address, date of birth and all other personal information that you have supplied previously. Simply asking you for this information, and comparing it to that on the screen, allows them to verify your identity.

So what happens if you forget your password? The administrator can RESET the password so the system sends YOU the new password without them seeing it.

If you are a member of a forum board then you will have seen this in action; if you forget your password then the forum board database will send you a new password to your email address.

Chapter 6 - How, and why, scammers will attempt to get your password

Hacking into a database is an extremely difficult thing to do. People will try though, NASA claims that over 20 people try to (unsuccessfully) hack into their systems daily.

The time and effort it takes would not justify the rewards. And why put in so much effort anyway? Isn't a crooks life supposed to be easier? So fraudsters take the easy route to get into a database – your username and password.
The only hurdle to this method is YOU! They need to trick you into telling them your account details; and they have lots of methods that they try.

Trying to trick you for your password is commonly known as 'Phishing'. If you are on the Internet you will receive an attempt sooner or later; I personally receive about five of these a day (so please don't get worried if you receive one, everyone does eventually).

For the first time in print (that I know of) I will show you what a Phishing email actually looks like and how to tell it's fraud.
All the emails that I show are ones that I have personally received over the past month.

The first examples I use target ebay, but ebay is not alone as a target for scammers. The lessons that I teach here can be applied to any, and all, Phishing emails.

Lastly, if ebay really do need to send you an email then they will send it to your ebay account as well. If you don't know if it is real then simply go to your web browser and type in 'www.ebay.com', if the email was real then it will appear in your account.
If the email is not in your ebay account then it is FAKE.

Ebay Phishing Example 1

From: eBay
Date: 02/06/06 01:00:39
To:
Subject: Complete your eBay Forum !

eBay sent this message to verify your information .
Your registered name is included to show this message originated from eBay . Learn more.
&nb sp;

Complete your eBay Forum

We regret to inform you that your eBay account could be suspended if you don't re-update your account information.To resolve this problems please complete the form.If your problems could not be resolved your account will be suspended for a period of 72 hours,after this period your account will be terminated.

- Expeditious removal of listings reported to eBay by over 5,000 intellectual property rights owners
- Specific, detailed warnings designed to deter the listing of potentially infringing items before a listing is posted on eBay
- Voluntary daily monitoring and removal by eBay of listings offering potentially counterfeit or otherwise infringing items
- Voluntary daily monitoring and removal by eBay of listings that violate eBay policies designed to prevent the listing of infringing items on eBay
- Suspension of repeat offenders
- Continuing efforts to identify and prevent previously suspended users from reregistering for eBay
- Cooperation with rights owners seeking personal information on alleged infringers.

However, because eBay is not an expert in your intellectual property rights, and cannot verify that sellers have the right to sell the millions of items they post on eBay each day, we need your help in identifying your status account to be sure that you are not one of those people who violate the eBay rules.We appreciate your support and understanding,as we work together to keep eBay a safe place to trade
Dear eBay Member,
To complete your eBay Forum, you must click the link below.

http://signin.ebay.com/id-verify

COMMENT: Looking at the *From:* area of the email it says '*eBay*', that's probably the easiest thing to change. I could send you an email and make the return address '*Genghis Khan*'.

The email uses the eBay logo, that is easy to do as well (a simple cut-and-paste).

The last thing here you need to know is the bottom line of "**http://signin.ebay.com/id-verify**" - this looks like the website you would go to if you clicked on it, but that is not always the case. There is no 'trick' to redirect a user to a different web site than the one they thought they were going to.

Note that the line at the top (in small print) says '*Your registered name is included to show this message originated from eBay*'. Well have another look as ***MY NAME DOESN'T***

APPEAR ANYWHWERE!; and if it did then that proves nothing as that information is easily found on ebay.

You're probably wondering 'how did they get my email address?'. It's very easy, with the right program a scammer can get everyone's email address from ebay.

Ebay Phishing Example 2

Password change required!

Dear sir,

We recently have determined that different computers have logged onto your eBay account, and multiple password failures were present before the logons. We strongly advice CHANGE YOUR PASSWORD.

If this is not completed by **February 10, 2006**, we will be forced to suspend your account indefinitely, as it may have been used for fraudulent purposes. Thank you for your cooperation.

Click here to Change Your Password

Thank you for your prompt attention to this matter.

We apologize for any inconvenience.

Thank you for using eBay!

COMMENT: Here the email asks you to click on the link in order to change your password. If you click on this you then go to a fake web site.
Again, if you think it is real then type 'www.ebay.com' in your web browser and make sure the email appears in your account.

DON'T EVER CLICK ON A LINK IN AN EMAIL.

A real email from eBay doesn't ask you to click on a link. EXCEPT (there is one exception, and one only) when you first open your ebay account you will be asked to click on the link included in the 'welcoming' email, this is in order to verify your account. Once your account has been verified you will **NEVER** be asked to verify it again.

Ebay Phishing Example 3

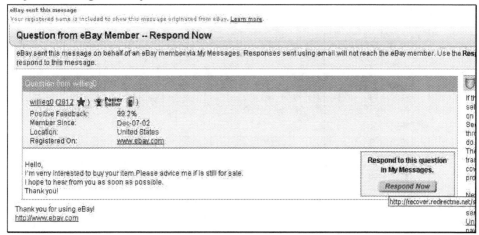

COMMENT: Nearly all of the scam emails are done to look the same as a real email from ebay. They will go to great lengths in order to make it look legitimate, even so far as to put the anti fraud ebay link in it!

This email looks exactly how a real 'ask a seller a question' email looks like. I receive about two or three real ones each day.

So now I'll teach a little trick - if you hover the mouse pointer over a web site link, and DO NOT click the mouse button, then the REAL web address appears!
In the screen shot above I have shown what happens. Where I have let the mouse pointer hover over the 'Respond Now' button (the mouse pointer goes missing when the link comes up), the box with 'http://recover.redirectme.net/security-ebay.com/signin.html' appears, this is the web site that you would go to if you clicked on the button (not where you thought!). Please don't try to access this website as it is a criminal website (safer to just stay away).

Ebay Phishing Example 4

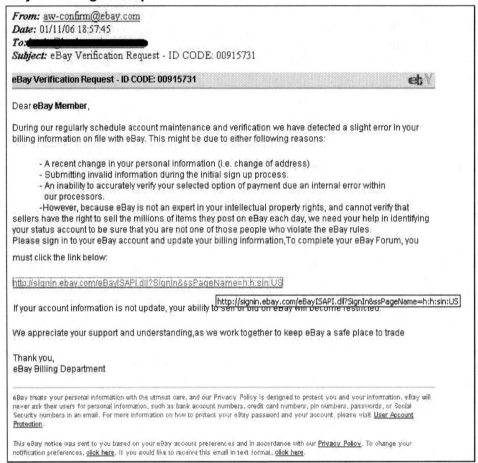

COMMENT: Every trick used so far is easy to do but this one is a bit harder as it uses JavaScript (a computer language) to mislead the user.

The link in the email says *'http://signin.ebay.com/ebayISAPS.dll?* etc etc' and if you hover the mouse pointer over the link it still says *'http://signin.ebay.com/ebayISAPS.dll? etc etc'!* But if you click on it you go to another site altogether!

Just remember that any email ebay sends you can be verified by going into your ebay account; if it's legitimate then there will be a message waiting for you.
IF THERE IS NO MESSAGE IN YOUR EBAY ACCOUNT THEN IT IS A FAKE.

Ebay Phishing Example 5

COMMENT: UH-OH! The last thing an ebay seller, including myself, wants is an angry customer; I had better hurry and see what has gone wrong.

This email (and this is the current trend) is very 'in your face' and demands attention; scammers want you to hit the 'Respond Now' button NOW!
Firstly, remember the trick about hovering your mouse pointer over the 'Respond Now' button – this shows the web site it links too (and it isn't ebay!).

Secondly, my registered name doesn't appear anywhere even though it says it does.

Thirdly, in the activity section it states that we have not dealt with each other within the last 90 days – yet in the email it is stated that the transaction happened two months ago!

Ebay Phishing example 6

> ### Dear eBay Seller ,
>
> We are about to delete all your Feedback earned for transactions on eBay because eBay buyer **baytree** accused you of eBay fraud. He told us that you never answer to his e-mail messages.
>
> Please <u>Sign In</u> as soon as possible so we can resolve this problem. If you don't reply to this message you can lose your feedback and maybe your eBay accoul `http://www.javacertificate.net/scwcd_21.htm`
>
> Thank you for your understanding.
>
> ebY

COMMENT: Really?? You're going to delete all my feedback because one person complained that I don't respond to their emails?

The first thing you need to learn is how ebay works, then you will realise that the above email (deleting a sellers feedback) cannot happen. There has never been an instance of ebay deleting any person's feedback (buyer or seller) even if their account is closed.

Ebay is like any business, and that includes having to deal with a certain amount of idiot buyers. There are about 25 people whose emails I refuse to answer (yet some of them still email me!).

They usually state how poor they are so they wish to buy a $100 item for $5, and could I please pay the postage?

If ebay really did delete previous feedbacks based on one bad experience then it would open up all sorts of abuse!

So what if you don't know how the system works (for example, you've only been a member for a week)?

Okay, lets take a look at it then – we hover the mouse pointer over the 'Sign In' button and '*www.javacertificate.net/scwcd_21.htm*' is displayed; not ebay at all.

Fake emails that claim to come from ebay actually look like real ones; this one doesn't even try!

Ebay Phishing example 7

Question from maxntytan

<u>maxntytan</u>(45 ☆)

Positive feedback:	97.9%
Member since:	15-Oct-04
Location:	AZ, United States
Registered on:	www.ebay.com

Item: **NEW NOKIA 8801 GSM VIDEO CAMERA TRI BAND CELL PHONE** (260065164569)
This message was sent while the listing was **active**.
maxntytan is a **potential buyer**.

Anything wrong with this phone? Just wondering why nobody has bid on it.

COMMENT: I don't sell phones, never have. Again, an attempt to get me to hit the 'Respond Now' button.

There is a second part to this scam; the 'Respond Now' button shows that you will go to ebay if you click on this link – WRONG!
Look carefully at the web link displayed - everything in front of the '=' sign is ignored and you will be taken to *http://cti-phil.com*.

FINAL WORD

I've said it before and I'll say it again - if ebay needs to send you an email they will send a copy to your ebay account. If you don't know if it is true or not then simply go to your web browser and type in www.ebay.com, if the email was real then the email will appear in your account.
If the email is not in your ebay account then it is FAKE. If you receive a fake email simply delete it.

19

Chapter 7 - What to do if you have given your password away

Don't feel bad if you've been duped. It has been reported that criminal gangs can make up to USD$60 million a year via Internet scams, so that makes a lot of victims.

Contact ebay (or who ever your account is with that has been stolen – this advice is not just for ebay accounts) and tell them that your account has been breached ('breached' is a diplomatic way of putting it).

They will then verify who you are, and then proceed to change the password of your account; this new password is sent to your email address (which means the ebay representative doesn't see it). This also means they can't give you the new password over the phone.

I have used ebay as an example here but it could just be easily your bank (or any other financial institute).

Please don't believe that these customer representatives will think you're an idiot; it happens daily. The major problem here is the victim admitting to what has happened; nobody can help you fix the problem until you tell them what has happened.
I know, from personal experience, that's it embarrassing to admit being a victim; get over it quickly today though or you may find your life savings missing tomorrow.

Chapter 8 - What to do if you have given details to a scammer

The scammer knows that time is their worst enemy; sooner or later the account will be shut down so they need to act straight away. The scammer will quickly transfer the money into a 'middle account', and then forwarded into their own account.

Please don't jump to the conclusion that the 'middle account' holder is a scammer (or works for the scammer); usually they are a victim of a different sort of scam which I call the 'work for us scam'.

Following is examples of the 'work for us scam' (please note that the following email is one that I have received and has not been edited or condensed in any way) –

'Work for us' scam example 1

Hello Sir/Madam,

We are a small and relatively Software Development and Outsourcing Company specializing in enterprise application development, system integration, corporate networks and other software solutions for business, finance, and for various types of problems. The company based in Ukraine but at this time we open new office in Bulgaria.

We?ve earned ourselves a reputation of a reliable and trustworthy partner working successfully with a number of West European and North American companies and providing them with reliable software development services in financial, telecom and media sectors. Also we are in search of new partners. Unfortunately we are currently facing some difficulties with receiving payments for our services. It usually takes us 10-30 days to receive a payment from your country and such delays are harmful to our business. We do not have so much time to accept every wire transfer and we can't accept cashier's checks or money orders as well. That's why we are currently looking for partners in your country to help us accept and process these payments faster.

If you are looking for a chance to make an additional profit you can become our representative in your country. As our representative you will receive 8% of every deal we conduct. Your job will be accepting funds in the form of wire transfers and check payments and forwarding them to us. It is not a full-time job, but rather a very convenient and fast way to receive additional income. We also consider opening an office in your country in the nearest future and you will then have certain privileges should you decide to apply for a full-time job.

This is an entry level opportunity in the field of financial services. Our financial professionals work with clients to help them achieve their many financial goals such as saving on taxes.

 Please if you are interested in transacting business with us we will be very glad. Please contact me for more information via softtechua@aim.com and send us the following information about yourself:

1. Your Full Name as it appears on your resume.
2. Education.
3. Your Contact Address.
4. Telephone/Fax number.
5. Your present Occupation and Position currently held.
6. Your Age

Please respond ASAP and we will provide you with additional details on how you can become our representative. Joining us and starting business today will cost you nothing and you will be able to earn a bit of extra money fast and easy.

Should you have any questions, please feel free to contact us at the address mentioned above. Looking forward to hearing from you.

Sincerely,
Victor Lesninsky
Director of Softtechua.

The irony of this email is that it is a real job offer - they really do want you to transfer money on their behalf.
The catch? The money you are receiving is coming from hijacked accounts. You are then passing the funds onto them – this is more commonly known as 'money laundering'.

So why do they need you to help transfer the funds? Because overseas money transfers can take up to five days to clear and can be reversed within that time; transferring the money to you first reduces the chance of a transaction being reversed before completion.

Example
Person A (we'll call him Adam) falls for the Phishing scam and gives their bank account details to Person F (we'll call him Frank the Fraudster), Frank then illegally accesses Adam's bank account and transfers all the money ($10,000 in this example) into Person B's bank account (Person B will be called Bruce, this is the 'middle account').
Bruce has fallen victim to the 'work for us' scam, and accepts the $10,000; he takes his 8% share ($800) and transfers the remaining $9,200 overseas to Frank.
The police arrive and Bruce is arrested for money laundering. After being found guilty (and he will be found guilty) he is ordered to repay the $10,000 to Adam. The money to Frank cannot be traced (as it was wire transfer) so Frank laughs all the way to his bank while Adam and Bruce both lose out (Bruce also goes to jail).

'Work for us' scam example 2

To the recipient

My name is Lee Finn Yoo I am the Sales Promotional Manager for Walk &Talk desktop wireless communicators.

We are the major distributors for desktop wireless communicators in Japan, our prime client bases covers most of Asia, but in recent times we expanded our sales network to North America, that being Canada and the United States. It is for this reason that we are looking for a reputable and trust worthy person to be our agent to make it more convenient for our clients to do business with us and to expedite the payment process.

In essence we are looking for an agent to receive payments on our behalf, because we do not have an account in the United States. Most of our North American clients like to pay by company check or casher's checks

If we deposit theses checks into our business bank account in Japan they usual put a 28th days hold or sometimes they might refuse to accept a check issued out of an American Bank especially if the clients bank does not have an affiliate bank here in Japan.

This payment problem has been great curse for concern forcing us to reluctantly suspend all our orders to the United States pending until we can find a clearing agent to receive payments on our behalf over there in the United States

For your role we are willing to compensate you with 10% of the total sale
You will withhold 10% and remit the balance to us as instructed by us. We usually get about four to six orders every month from our North American market, each order varies from $4000 any where up to $50,000 or more, depending on the order. Our clearing agent in Australia can usually earns about $1000 to $4000 USD depending on the sales volume of that month.

With very little effort on your part this is a good extra income potential for you, it will not be necessary to vacate your current job, so this can be an additional income opportunity.

Please Note that this is not a multi level or network marketing scheme, you will not be required to pay any joining fee or be ask to get others involved or be mandated to purchase any inventory. NEED TO BOLD

Also you are not required to do any selling or cold calling. On our

23

part we send out hundreds of product information flyers every month to businesses and retailer in the United States and Canada, hence we generate our own leads. When we secure a purchases order our North American Sales liaison in Canada will contact you to arrange for the buyers to make payments to you as our clearing agent in the United States.

In a nutshell we pay you for your assistants in any transaction that we procure from our North American Clients, It is that simply!!!

In case you are curious to know how I got your name and address, I obtained it from a general Internet name and address search.

If this proposal is of interest to you.

Email me at: mr_leefinn1@yahoo.co.jp

it is better that we communicate via e-mail because of the different time zones and also because my English is very bad, when you e-mail me I can get someone to translate your reply to me, and my reply to you If you have any question feel free ask them in your reply, also once you reply I will give you our web site so that you can learn more about us and our products.

If you must call me you can
556676 Nine to Five Japan time

In Japan our word is our bond all we ask of you is that you share the same sentiment.
I look forward to doing business with you in the near future.

Yours truly,

Lee Finn Yoo (BSC. Hon)
Sales Promotional Manager

COMMENT: I'm in Australia, the job is offered to North Americans while the business is in Japan.

'Work for us' scam example 2

Alfa Oil and Gas Company seek representatives and partners in South/North America,
Europe, Asia, and Australia, for expantion, investment and debt recovery.

a) As a representative of Alfa Oil and Gas in your location, you be entitled to a 10% commission.
b) AS a global investor, expantion and debt recovery partner, you shall be entitled to a 22% share
for investment funding and debt recovery.

Please state the option that best suits you and provide details:

Your full names
Company name
Your residential Address
Your Telephone and fax Number

Charles Arthur.
Phone: +447902713856
Email: deskofcharles_alfaoilgas@yahoo.com

COMMENT: This example is simple and effective, but fraud just the same.

There are many more examples of the 'Work for us' scam but they are all the same; they
will pay you a percentage of the money that you help them transfer.
It comes back to the old saying 'There is no such thing as a free lunch'; if an offer sounds
too good to be true then it usually is.

Chapter 9 - Identity Theft

You've probably heard about it before but have you wondered how it all really works?

Identity theft is simply a case of a person imitating someone else. The amount of personal damage that can be done is devastating; and not just short term either - it can have ramifications years down the track.

Identity theft is a lot easier than most people would like to think. It is very easy to obtain personal information from a victim if they are unaware that they are giving it away.

The Nigerian letter scam asks you for your personal information in order to prove your honesty (the irony). Lottery scams ask for your personal information in order to verify your identity. Telephone marketers (that purport to be from your financial institute) ask you to verify who you are before they discuss your account. This person might be real but the only way to know this is to ring them back (there is NO reason why a bank representative will not allow you to ring them back in order to verify who they are).

So how is this information used? Scammers will fill out loan forms, in the victims' name, to hundreds of financial institutions within a twenty-four hour period.
The reason it is all done within twenty-four hours is so the financial institutions don't know that the same person has filled out hundreds of applications. Once you fill in an application (any financial application) every other financial institute knows about it the next day – so all the paperwork needs to be done on the same day by the scammer.

The next step is for the financial institution to verify your identity.
All they do is call the victims place of work in order verify that they work there; the problem is that they don't speak to the victim, they speak to the finance department.
Once the financial institutes have verified that the victim does indeed work there they will then attempt to verify all the information on the application form. The finance department will VERIFY all this because it is *all true* (remember that the victim gave the scammers all this information in the initial scam).
At this time it needs to be noted that the financial institutions (and the victims finance department) have no idea that a scam is in progress.

I know how this works because my mother is an accountant and receives these phone calls about once a week. She verifies the caller but has no idea if the loan is a scam or not. It's not in her job description to check out each workers personal life in order to double check these sorts of details.

So, the scammer gets the loan and asks for the money in CASH. If this is accepted then the scammer will send a person around to the bank to pick the money up (this is when scammers usually get caught by police because it is the only time that the scammer actually shows themselves in public).

If the scammer walks away with the money then they have successfully completed the scam; the first the victim knows about it is when they receive a bank statement in the mail, this gives the scammer about three days to get away.

There is no limit to how bad this scam can get; if the scammer can keep borrowing money then they will. When the victims' credit rating is ruined then the scammer simply moves onto their next victim.

This scam also causes a lot of problems in the future if the victim ever wishes to take out a loan because of their (now) ruined credit rating.

PART 2 – EBAY

Whether you love it or hate it ebay is currently the biggest auction site in the world. It is also one of the biggest web sites in the world (Alexa© has it ranked as the fourteenth most visited web site in the world at the time I researched for this book).

The concept of ebay is simple; you place an item on ebay to which people around the world proceed to bid on – when the auction finishes you collect payment from the winning bidder and send the item.

In 2006 ebay had around US$50 Billion dollars worth of goods traded on it; you cannot have that sort of money traded without criminals taking notice.
The scams that these criminals attempt on ebay range from the ridiculous to the very good. You may think that the ridiculous attempts wouldn't work but they do; there are approximately 3,000 new users every day who need time to learn how the system works, in this time they wouldn't know if an email is from ebay or if it's a badly worked scam email.

The following chapters show scams that target ebay buyers, ebay sellers and ebay auctions.
If you are serious, or not, about trading on ebay then you need to be ready to receive fake emails.

Chapter 10 - Shill bidding

This is one area of ebay that can be policed and is cracked down on hard when discovered. Shill bidding is simply the act of a seller using dummy bids to boost the price on their own auctions. Dummy bids can be made from a sellers second account (nobody is stupid enough to use their own ebay account to bid on their own item – having said that I bet it has happened) or getting someone else to bid on the item (wife/husband for example).

The ebay bidding is done by what is called 'proxy bidding'. What this means is that when you put your maximum price that you are willing to bid into the system it will then bid on the item up until you are either the highest bidder OR you are at your maximum bid – it won't go over the maximum price that you specified.

Example

Sue is the seller, Harry is Sue's Husband and Brian is the potential buyer.

Sue puts a second hand laptop onto ebay and starts the auction at $1, she hopes for around $600. Brian bids first and offers $500; because of the proxy bidding system it comes up that Brian is the highest bidder at $1 (there are no other bidders at the moment).

Sue is not happy about selling her laptop for $1 so she gets her husband to bid, Harry bids $10,000 (shill bidders bid way too high at the start). Now the system shows that Harry is the highest bidder at $501 ($1 more than Brian's highest bid, remember that the system stops upping Harry's bid when he is the highest bidder).
Now Sue can see that Brian's highest bid was $500, so Harry now retracts his bid of $10,000 (the excuse is 'I meant to put in $100.00 but forgot the decimal point'). Now Harry bids $499 to push Brian's winning bid to $500.

So what happens if the seller shill bids and accidentally wins the item? They simply offer the loser a second chance offer.

Shill Bidding suspension example 1

SB NOTICE: eBay Registration Suspension - Shill Bidding

Hello,

This email is to notify you that your account has been suspended for a minimum of 7 days due to violation of our Shill Bidding Policy.

Shill Bidding is bidding that artificially increases an item's price or apparent desirability. Shill Bidding is prohibited on eBay. Information on eBay's Shill Bidding Policy can be found at:

http://pages.ebay.com/help/policies/seller-shill-bidding.html

Your account has been fou[http://dutedreaq.pochta.ru/dainmmcontusafacsieubankktdreaq.aspx]ed accounts:

naw017

You are prohibited from using eBay in any way (including use of other existing accounts or registering new accounts) during your suspension.

Any auctions you currently have open have been cancelled. Please note tha t any fees incurred for these auc

This is an email that tells you that your account has been suspended. This is well done as it links to the rules of ebay, but if you click on it (in order to see which rule you have 'broken') then you are taken to a false web site.

My account has never been suspended so I don't know if this email looks real or not. Things to take note of are –
1. The email is 'from' a fellow ebay member (chips2481); an email that suspended your account would come from ebay themselves.
2. The email has been sent to 'undisclosed-recipients', which means it was sent to hundreds of users. It is a bulk scam email.
3. I have been suspected of dealing with *naw017* who I have never heard off.
4. Lastly, the web address link goes to a fake web site. Note that the '.ru' means that the web site is in Russia.
5. It starts with 'Hello'; a real email from ebay uses your name – 'Dear James'.

Chapter 11 - Retracted bids

The previous chapter showed a method of how retracted bids can be used to push the price of an item up (Shill bidding). Now we explore another method of how an unscrupulous buyer can push the price down by using the same method!

When looking though ebay you are usually looking for an item at a fair price (your belief of what a fair price is anyway). If you are searching for an item that you believe is overpriced then you will not be inclined to stick around in order to bid for it.
So an item can be overpriced for a long time and then in the final minutes of the auction the price collapses because the highest bidder retracts their bid. Because of ebay's proxy bidding system the winning bid is now a lot lower.

Example

We'll imagine that things went wrong in the previous example and Sue is selling her laptop again.

Sue is the seller, Brian is the potential buyer and Rory is the Retracting bidder. Brian and Rory are working together while Sue doesn't know either of them.

Sue puts the Laptop onto ebay again, starts the bidding at $1 (again) and expects around $600 for it. This time Brian bids $2,000 for the laptop; because of the proxy bidding system Brain's current bid comes in at $1 as he is the only bidder so far, Brian knows that he will win the Laptop for $1 if no-one else bids, so he needs to make sure that there are no more bidders.
Rory then bids $2,500 on the laptop. Now the proxy bidding system shows that Rory is the highest bidder at $2,001 (Brian had put in $2,000, the system stops upping Rory's bids when it is greater than Brian's highest offer).

Sue is extremely happy with this predicament as she looks to be getting $2,001 for a laptop that she expected $600 for; other potential buyers, who are looking for laptops, don't bid on it because the price is too high, so there are no other bids.
With one minute of the auction to go Rory retracts his $2,500 bid; the proxy system now shows that Brian is the highest bidder at $1 (remember that there were no other bidders). Unless someone is watching in the last 30 seconds, and bids on the item, then the winning bid will be Brian's $1.

Chapter 12 - Postage costs

Out of all the scams on ebay this one probably has the most false accusations. This is also the easiest scam to spot.

Most buyers believe that the price of the stamp should be the cost of postage, and that's how much they are going to pay.
There have been situations where a buyer has only paid the cost of the stamp (or what they perceive the cost to be) which creates a stand off position – the seller refuses to send the item until the buyer pays the outstanding postage amount while the buyer refuses to pay anymore because they believe they have paid enough.

Postage cost also includes the cost of packing materials, boxes, tape and time spent.
I personally never charge for the time spent packing an item, but I can see why some people do. A lot of time can be spent properly packing a large, fragile item; and the buyer usually doesn't appreciate this. But if the item turns up broken then the buyer does notice!
I once bought a poster on ebay and when it arrived it was completely trashed, I opened it only to discover glass everywhere. My wife has received postcards with scratch marks on them and posters that were bent in half.
My rule of thumb for packing? Pack it to the point where you could kick the package like a football and not damage what is inside. I have heard of stories of parcels being kicked across the floor at the mail-sorting centre, so make sure the package is prepared for it!

The other side of this is those who make a living out of postage charges. By selling items cheaper than your competitor you can sell more, and then overcharge on the postage in order to make a profit. I did once have a competitor who did this, they were gone within 3 months as nobody would deal with them (but it did damage my sales in the short term).
It's not a long-term strategy but there are always those who try it.

So what is a reasonable charge for postage? Depends on the item! For my items I usually charge double the cost of the stamp - and nobody has ever complained about that. Again, it depends on the items. A fragile item could be a lot more because of the extra packaging.

The worst case I have seen is a $5 video camera with a postage fee of $80, but it also had to be insured at the buyers' expense, which was another $25 – when the item arrived the stamp was $25 (it was from overseas).
In this case the seller did offer a refund but you needed to pay the return postage cost ($25); then you were only refunded the purchase price ($5), which is in accordance with ebay's return policy.

Chapter 13 - Change of Address

On average the Australian family moves house every 7 years.
I have about 1,000 Australian customers so, on average, 12 customers move each month.
About 3 of them will update their contact details on ebay but that leaves a lot of customers that I have to follow up on.
About once a month I will have items returned to me, then I have to ring the customer who usually hasn't updated their phone number! Luckily most people have mobile phones so I can contact them that way.
But the odd package still remains unclaimed (I have one in front of me as I write this chapter).

This is a normal occurrence of business. What you need to learn is how to tell a real claim from a false one. If you feel that something is wrong then simply ring the person to verify their details.

If a customer has moved it doesn't necessarily mean that they are dishonest.

If a customer gets a neighbour to pick up their mail from the old house, and then redirects it, the customer may then claim that they never received the item.
The postal system takes no responsibility for this as they delivered it to the address specified; so unless you know the neighbour (or whoever they got to pick it up) then you have no way of knowing if they received it or not.

I have had a courier deliver a box to the wrong address to which they refused to go back and redeliver. The courier company believed that they had delivered the box, even though it was to the wrong address. So make sure you are ready to take responsibility when things go wrong.

The most common address scam is people stealing an account and changing details so the items are sent to a false address. These criminals will steal credit card numbers, buy as many items as they can and have them all sent to the bogus address.
When the payments are reversed (because of the fraud) all the sellers would like their items back; the police are sent to investigate but only find innocent victims.
The trick is for the criminal to wait at the address for the parcel to arrive and then take it before the owners arrive home from work.
It is not uncommon for a scammer to use a next door neighbours address for this scam so they can hear the postal worker deliver the mail; if the neighbour catches the scammer then they can point to the name on the parcel and show that the address was wrong (remember that scammers don't use their real names, they say it was delivered for a friend).

Chapter 14 - Refunds

Do you have to give refunds? Legally 'yes' if the item that arrived doesn't match the description, but 'no' if the customer is simply unhappy with their purchase.

For customer relation purposes most sellers offer full refunds if the customer is not happy (I always have, these days most of my customers are repeat customers so it works out in the long term).

First (and this really is a no brainer) wait for the items to be returned before you refund their payment.

I sent a playing card to Singapore that turned up damaged to which I offered a full refund. They accepted the refund as store credit and bought other cards from me. I then offered to send them the new cards first so they could use the envelope to return the damaged cards to me (if they changed the contents of the envelope and then marked it 'return to sender' then there is no return postage cost). It was all agreed too. I sent the new cards but never received the other cards back.

I lost around $50 of cards in order to save the buyer $1.50 in postage fees.

Another reason you want the items returned first is to check if they are in fact the items that you sent in the first place.

I have heard a story of an antique watch being sent back with the timepiece replaced with a cheap copy, but that story pales in comparison to the buyer who sent back a ring after replacing the ruby with a cough lolly.

What do you do in this situation? Get the police involved straight away, this is fraud and it is a sure bet that this person has done this before. In this case the payment is probably fraudulent anyway, scammers rarely use 'one method' to defraud – every trick they know is used in order to maximise profits (and paying for an item with a stolen credit card, stealing the real item and then getting a refund really makes a profitable transaction).

If things do go wrong then don't expect to get the real item back; but if you haven't given a refund your loses shouldn't be too bad. When you are dealing with a scammer you need to remember that their sense of logic is very warped – to them if you don't call the police then you obviously didn't think it was an illegal transaction, if you do call the police then they believe the illegal gains they made makes up for the inconvenience YOU caused THEM, so they don't see why they should have to repay the money.

NEVER try to reason with a scammer in order to try to get your money back, they will simply sit there and try to convince you that YOU are the scammer. Simply let the courts take care of them.

Chapter 15 - Linking to web sites off ebay

According to the rules of ebay you may only link to web sites off ebay if it provides more information on the item. For example, if you are selling an iPod then you may link to the official iPod web site so people can get more information on the product before making a bid.
You may not link to another web site in order to sell the product for a lower cost; this is so you cannot circumvent ebay fees.

This rule is fairly well policed by ebay but when it is exploited it is really exploited!!

The main reason for the seller to try and get a buyer off ebay is so the buyer is no longer covered by ebay policies; if this happens then you cannot leave negative feedback if the transaction goes bad!

Ebay tries very hard to get buyers to pay with Paypal, that way the transaction can be traced. If the transaction is done off ebay then the buyer may wish to use other methods of payment that, usually, can't be traced.

So how is this done if ebay police the policy fairly hard? Via sheer weight of numbers and 'brute force'.
The best example is to type in 'wow gold' in the ebay search engine and you will find hundreds of items. 'wow' stands for 'World of Warcraft', a very successful online game run by Blizzard corporation. (Note that Blizzard is a very reputable company and has no involvement with any ebay scams.)
The items listed in ebay under 'wow gold' are for people to buy gold (the official in-game currency) for use in the game (you are not buying a physical object).
To pay for this you need to go to a separate web site and give them your credit card details; if you had used paypal they would never see your credit card number.

The reason these ebay accounts keep operating is that they are set up with false details (they use credit cards that were illegally gained from customers).
When ebay shuts their accounts down (and they usually do very quickly, this is an easy scam to spot) the scammers simply open a new account and set the listings up again. It seems to be a never-ending circle; I've been watching it for go on for about 3 years and it doesn't look like ending any time soon.

This scam not only effects 'wow' but also nearly every other online game. I must also add that any seller that wants you to go off ebay to buy (or pay for) an item must be viewed with suspicion.

Chapter 16 - Wire transfers

It used to be that scammed money was transferred via _Western Union_ only as it is totally untraceable. This method is now so well known that people get suspicious when this is the only method of payment that the seller will allow.
Note that _Western Union_ advises its members to only send funds to people that they personally know.

These days fake Paypal accounts are set up and then closed down when the money is received. Don't assume Paypal covers you if you are defrauded in this instance - I'll discuss this more in the Paypal section.

Scammers spend most of the day going through ebay looking for high priced items (no use scamming for small amounts of money, might as well go straight for the 'jackpot').
When a scammer finds a high priced auction that has just finished they will then proceed to email all the bidders. The winner of the auction will be emailed to say that the money is to be transferred via wire transfer; the hope here is that the winning bidder will send the money before they realise that they are being scammed.
If the winning bidder asks why paypal (or bank transfer, or any other method) cannot be used to pay for this item, although it states it is allowed in the description, the scammer will reply that their paypal account is currently frozen or their bank account is no longer current.
Even after the real seller contacts the winning buyer to ask where the funds are the winner may not realise that they have been scammed, they may believe that the seller has stolen their funds! This creates a huge problem all round (meanwhile the scammer has absconded with the funds, they don't care about the problems they have caused).
The seller continues to demand their money while the buyer continues to demand that their item be sent as they believe they have paid for it.

Don't think the scammer only targets the winning bidder either.
They realise that there is only about a 2% chance of this scam working. So they proceed to email all the other, unsuccessful, bidders at the same time. This email states that the winning bidder has pulled out of the auction and so they are offering the item for a lower amount (this is commonly known as 'a second chance offer').
The scammer then gets the losing bidder to wire transfer the money, to which the scammer makes off with. The losing bidder then emails the seller to ask when the item will arrive and the seller goes insane (trust me on this one).

When I started on ebay about one in five customers accepted a 'second chance offer' from me, but I haven't sold anything using this method for over two years because of the suspicion it now causes.

Chapter 17 - Auction Interference

Ever wondered why an item got a price that seemed really low? Or why several buyers suddenly withdraw their bids on an item at the same time?

There is a good chance that *auction interference* has taken place.

Auction interference is exactly what it sounds like; someone is interfering with the running of an auction.
The most common way is for the villain to email all the bidders to tell them that the seller is a crook; most people will simply withdraw their bids instead of finding out if it is true or not.
Unfortunately a good reputation is like a house of cards; one slanderous person can bring it all crashing down.

Complaints can be made to ebay about this interference but by then all the customers will have gone elsewhere and the damage has been done.

The two types of people who will do this scam are your competitors or someone who wants your item for a cheap price. The scammers objective here is to get rid of the other bidders in order to win the item cheaply.

Unfortunately there is not much that can be done if you have been targeted by this scam. All you can do is try to get a copy of the email that was sent to your potential buyers and then decide on a course of action.
I realise that I am not much help here as I haven't personally been a victim of this scam (yet).

Chapter 18 - Allegations of price fixing and overpricing

Using a second account (or person) to inflate auction prices is the scam more commonly known as 'shill bidding'; allegations are the other way around, it's an attempt by a buyer to blackmail the seller in order to get the item for a lower price.

It is possible to get a persons account suspended simply by launching several complaints at the same time. If this is done then the ebay system will mark the seller as a troublemaker and the account may be automatically suspended.

Ebay's policy seems to be that if they can't investigate the claim straight away then the account is suspended until someone can; this is especially true if several complaints are lodged by different accounts at the same time against the same person.

Scammers have lots of accounts so they can lodge several complaints at the same time and get their victim shut down until it can be investigated, until that time the victim is helpless.

An allegation is simply someone emailing you complaining that you are overpricing an item; they will also accuse you of shill bidding (rarely they don't, although the first time I was accused of overpricing an item I wasn't accused of shilling).

The buyer then offers you a 'fair price' (and this is REALLY open to interpretation) or else they will report you to ebay. Where they get their 'fair price' from is anyone's guess, for all we know they could roll a dice in order to get this amount; usually they offer the lowest price the item has ever sold for on ebay.

The first time I received this email the item was in the middle of an auction that had pushed the item well over the price I was expecting (you win some, you lose some). I politely emailed back and said that an auction was the best way to find out the price of an item; and why should I sell the item to them cheaply when someone (in this case, five other people) were willing to pay a lot more.

That was a mistake.

I have stated before that scammers have a warped sense of logic and that there is no point in talking to them; this person was no exception as I got an abusive email in response. The only part of the email I can remember is that I was accused of communist behaviour, which was ironic as communists don't allow market forces to dictate the price of an item.

As with most other scams, simply ignore the email.

Chapter 19 - Early offers

This isn't a scam, but as a seller on ebay you need to know about this.

I've had early offers for lots of items, and I have never accepted one. If the offer was reasonable I would think about it but in every case it has been too low.
The buyers who make the early offers know the true value of an item. The offer is made early in the auction so the price is not too high and their offer looks good.
From experience the early offer will always be beaten by the final auction price, so don't be tempted to sell early.

I have heard of legitimate reasons for people wishing to buy an item early. Dresses for a formal that weekend, concert tickets so travel can be organised, costumes for a party that is coming up etc
Wether the story is true or not is not the point; the point is that you, as the seller, are entitled to sell the item for what people are willing to pay. If you still wish to sell early then make sure you are happy with the price being offered.
If you do sell early then make sure they are paying for the postage costs as well.

The stories to look out for are the buyers that plead poverty and try to convince you that they can't afford the item. If they are really in dire financial straits then why are they trying to buy an iPod? When I was a poor university student my last couple of dollars went towards food, not DVD players.
I don't believe most of the stories that potential buyers tell me.

I have had a customer buy an item from me and then said it was an accident, they didn't want my item as they didn't know what it was.
Yeah?
Too bad anyone on ebay can view another persons bidding history, I pointed that out to her and that she had bought a cheaper version ten minutes after winning mine. I nullified the transaction anyway, no use having an unhappy customer.
You will find it common that buyers tell you that they cannot complete the transaction because the account holder is dead, injured, hospitalised etc only to find out later that the 'dead' buyer is still purchasing items, and paying for them.

Chapter 20 - Price guides

The most useless item on the Internet is a so-called price guide. They are the bane of most sellers; especially sellers like myself who work in a niche market.

The amount of trouble I have stemming from price guides drives me crazy.
"My price guide states that your item is worth $60."
"Why do you charge $12 for a card when my price guide says it's worth for $9?"

My first complaint is that price guides assume that the whole world trades in United States currency. US$9 is the same (at the time of writing) as AUS$12 but I get accused of overcharging when I want $12 for it while they believe it's worth $9 (the email was from a US buyer so I had to assume they meant US dollars).

One thing Australia and the United States has in common is their free market economies, which simply means that I can sell an item for whatever price I want.
Price guides show the average price of how much an item sold for in the last week (or month or year - whatever the time span may be). Yet a lot of people seem to think that a price guide shows how much it SHOULD be sold for which causes problems.
In my niche market prices can fluctuate wildly; a game card that was useless one night may be tomorrow's big thing. An example is a card called 'Juzam Djinn', when it first came out (1995) it was seen to be a hindrance, so the people who received one threw it in the bin! These days they are valued at around $200, if you can find one.

Chapter 21 -Drop Shippers and Distributors

Drop shippers allow you to sell their products directly from the warehouse.
In theory it sounds great, you –
- Find a drop shipper
- Source what the drop shipper has in stock
- Put it on ebay
- Sell it
- Collect the money
- Transfer money to the drop shipper who sends the item to the buyer

This is not illegal or immoral but it is very hard to make money from this system; the fact that these people tell you that it is easy money makes it a scam in my book.

Lots of things go wrong here, lets look at them one step at a time.

Find a drop shipper

This is the easiest part as drop shipper lists can be found all over ebay. Prices range from $1 for a list of three thousand distributors, up to $800 for a particular digital camera drop shipper out of Singapore.
Your first problem is that everyone can, and will, buy these drop shipper lists because they are freely available. Whatever product you decide to sell will be sold by at least ten other people that are drawn to the, supposedly, easy life of selling on behalf of a drop shipper. Competition may be healthy but too much competition will erode any profit margins.
These drop shippers will tell you that the prices are wholesale – that's wrong as I've seen 'wholesale' prices that were more expensive than my local department store – add on the postage cost and you are really getting ripped off.

Source what the drop shipper has in stock

Unless you arrive at the warehouse you have no way of knowing what is actually there.

They may be a drop shipper on behalf of other drop shippers and not have the stock themselves; this will multiply all other problems.

If the drop shipper has the item that you wish to sell there is still no guarantee that the item will be there once you have sold it; I have never come across a drop shipper that puts items aside for you when you are trying to sell them.

It is common to sell an item on ebay only to have the drop shipper tell you that 'we currently don't have any in stock, but we are expecting more in about a month"; meanwhile your buyer is expecting the item within seven days. You have no choice but to refund the money and accept the negative feedback that goes with it.

Put it on ebay

Now you put the item on ebay and wait for the item to sell. There is not much to do at this time but dream of your future wealth.

Sell it

This is where reality hits for the most people.

Some sellers believe that if you sell an item for more than you have bought it for then you have made a profit; this fails to take into account other expenses such as postage/handling and ebay costs (just to name a few).

Drop shippers will tell you that a 5% gross profit margin is good; but what you really need is at least a 50% gross profit margin. Think about it, you make 5% profit and your ebay fees are around 3.5% - ebay makes more money from the transaction than you do, yet you still have to pay all your other expenses from your remaining 1.5%.

I have tried drop shippers and have never been able to make any money. I don't know anyone who has made money from an item that has a 5% gross profit margin.

My rule of thumb is that I need a 100% gross profit to make a living.

Collect the money

Collecting the money from the buyer is the easiest part. Just remember that if anything goes wrong it is you who are responsible because you received the money (more on that in the next section).

Transfer money to the drop shipper who will send the item straight to the buyer

If the buyer receives the item (if they receive it at all) and the item is faulty then they will want their money back (or the item is not what they expected and they would like a refund), then YOU must refund the money – not the drop shipper; they will refund the money when they receive the item back (if at all).

With a 5% profit margin you can't afford this, and by the time you get everything sorted out you will lose a lot more than your tiny profit.

From experience about 2% of parcels go missing in the postal system. Note that the drop shipper will not reimburse you for lost parcels.

I worked it out one day that if one parcel goes missing with a 5% profit margin then you need to sell another 19 items simply to cover the cost of that missing item. Good luck in making a living with that profit margin.

Personal Experience

Yes I have done this; I paid a Singaporean drop shipper an eighty dollar fee in order to sell Digital cameras.

I paid the money and was given a password for their web site. I sat there for two hours doing research before I realised that I was reading the recommended selling prices, now it looked good. The average selling price was about 3% less than what my competitors were selling the same items for on ebay, and about 15% less than the department stores.

I quickly emailed back to explain that I had been sent the wrong price list, and could I please be sent the wholesale price list.

They explained that what I had was the wholesale prices and that they were very competitive. They also explained that I should be aiming for a 5% gross profit margin on all their items.

Here's where I think it's a scam – they are telling me that their prices are 'very competitive' when I know that they are not. There are not too many items in this world that you can make a profit from a 5% margin.

My local department store offers me a 10% discount if I pay with cash. Remember I said that the 'wholesale' price was 15% less than this store, so I wouldn't have saved much more than if I bought it from the drop shipper. But I personally would have spent the little more extra because if something goes wrong with the camera I can simply take it back to the store and exchange it.

Another thing I noticed was my competitors on ebay were starting some of their auctions at $1 for very expensive digital cameras; if I wanted to spend the time I could have offered very low prices on these items and won them for less than the drop shipper was offering them. This would cause the ebay seller to LOSE money (because I know how much they got them for) – but that wouldn't have been my problem.

I only ever sold one camera, and that was too myself to check out the quality and speed of delivery.

The quality was okay but the package sat in the couriers' office for two weeks because NOBODY TOLD ME that it was there ready to pick up! I have a post box but the courier won't deliver to post box numbers, so it sat in their office – but I wasn't notified. The drop shipper was notified about this but they took another two weeks to tell me.

Distributors

If you are buying items and then selling them via ebay then you are a retailer, retailers buy from distributors who buy from the manufacturer. A drop shipper is simply another middle man.

So what you need to do is skip the drop shipper part altogether and find the distributor.

So how do you find a good distributor and not just a drop shipper in disguise? By checking out their terms and conditions. If a distributor wants you to buy a minimum of $2,000 worth of goods at any one time then you are on the right track; if there is no minimum purchase amount then consider yourself warned.

Chapter 22 - Selling on behalf of others (trading assistant)

The single biggest scam I have been involved with was another powerseller who was a trading assistant. I'll explain the details at the end of this chapter.

A trading assistant is simply a person who sells items on ebay on behalf of others.

I've been a trading assistant and was screwed over big time – never will you find it more important to have a signed contract.
This contract is to protect you from unscrupulous sellers - that's right, the enemy is now behind you as well.

Goods owner

A trading assistant will sell on behalf of the goods owner, and this presents your first lot of problems.

When I started as an assistant I sold on behalf of friends, and learned a few lessons along the way.

The first item I sold for a friend was a piece of antique furniture. We agreed on a minimum price that it would sell for, but seven days through the ten-day auction she decided that she didn't want to sell it so we withdrew it from auction. She didn't reimburse my ebay fees.

The second item I sold was the antique furniture piece again (we were still friends at this point). We agreed to the terms again and this time she said she was serious. The reserve price was $2,000 and when the auction finished the piece had reached $2,100. She reneged on the deal as she realised that she didn't wish to sell it for that price, even though it was higher than the reserve we had agreed on. She (again) refused to reimburse me my ebay fees.
We haven't spoken since.

My third item was a mobile phone – which didn't work. Luckily at this stage I had decided to make a rule that all items had to be at my house before they were put on ebay; if I hadn't seen the phone first then I wouldn't have known that it didn't work. When I asked about this his response was 'I can't get it to work, maybe whoever buys it can'.
If the description says that the item works perfectly then the buyer won't be happy if they receive a faulty item.
I refused to sell the mobile phone.

At this stage I believed I had the experience to sell on behalf of strangers, so I made a few rules to help me in my new enterprise. They were simple –

- Goods to reside at my house during the auction (GOLDEN RULE)
- Contracts to be signed and adhered too
- If the goods owner wishes to withdraw the goods from auction then there is a small cancellation fee

This is one case where the rules cannot be simple; all the problems that I encountered while being an assistant would never have occurred if I had made a better contract. Legal documents are long and boring for a reason, to take into account any variations that may happen; people will fight over the most minor point if it means an extra dollar. If it's in writing then there are no arguments.

Side point – I have a friend who opened a 'bricks and mortar' store. Before starting, he signed a 20-page contract with the landlord which he thought covered everything. When he moved in there was no rubbish bins because it wasn't in the contract.

So now I started selling on behalf of others as an assistant (not just friends).

Everything started well; I gained a few clients who gave me several items to sell. Some of them were not happy about having the goods residing at my house during the auction but I stuck with my golden rule.

Selling the items wasn't the problem; it was when paying the client (the goods owner) that the problems started.
First problem was from an old lady whose book sold for $250; she expected $200 so you would think she would be happy. She argued that she should only pay a commission on the $200, and that the extra $50 was a bonus for her.
We argued over the finer points of the contract where I explained that the commission was to be paid on the final price; well, that wasn't her interpretation of the contract, she believed that the commission was to be paid on the reserve price.
I was threatened with legal action so I conceded.

Next problem was for a gentleman who I sold a computer part for at $1800; the reserve price was $1,500 but he was expecting $2,000.
My fee was 30% of the final selling price if the item sold for under $2,000 (I have a sliding scale for my fees). He argued that I had told him that my fee was to be 25% of the final selling price.
I pointed to the contract and explained that I take 25% if the item sells for more than $2,000, but this item had sold for under that amount so I charge 30%; he wouldn't accept this and said that I had quoted him 25% (it was going in circles here).
Again I was threatened with legal action so I, again, conceded.

The third problem was a $3,000 sound system. I heard the sound system in operation at the clients' house but never checked it myself.

The item was sold and delivered only for it to be revealed that the remote control didn't work; it would cost $250 to replace.

I rang the client up and explained this and his answer was 'so? What's it got to do with me?' I explained that the item was sold on the basis that it was fully operational and it wasn't.

His answer was simple – "That's your problem, not mine. Take me to court if you are not happy." He then proceeded to hang up on me.

Notice that in all three cases there were threats of legal action? These are the sorts of people you are dealing with. They will argue over the most minor point of a contract; I would hate to imagine what would have happened if there was no contract in the first place.

I came to the conclusion that there is a reason these people use trading assistants to sell their goods – they can't sell it themselves on ebay. Possibly they have had their account suspended or received too much negative feedback. Whatever the reason, they simply can't sell their own items.

They believe that they can mistreat an assistant because, to them, the assistant knows it's a business, and in a business you need to keep the customer happy. If they pulled the same stunts on other ebay users they would be rudely told where to go.

Two against One

At the start of this chapter I said that one of the worst scams I was personally involved in was with a trading assistant.

Life is hard enough against the amount of scams out there at any one time; but when two scammers gang up it makes life very hard.

I must state first that when I said I was involved in the scam that I wasn't the scammer or the scammed; I was one of the bidders and I knew the trading assistant. The item was also in my niche market so I was asked to verify the item before it was put up for auction.

A person approached the assistant and asked them to sell a collection of cards ('Magic the Gathering', it's a card game); the assistant agreed and worked out a contract with the client.

I will add here that my golden rule was not followed; the assistant didn't have the cards reside at her house.

The final price of the auction was $5,000 (I pulled out at $3,000), which I thought was a fair price for this collection. The buyer paid the money to the assistant; the assistant took out their $1,200 fee and transferred the remaining $3,800 to the client. From here the client should have sent the item to the buyer via registered post.

A month later the buyer claimed that they never got the item and went for a refund via Paypal; paypal quickly refunded the $5,000 without consulting the assistant.

The assistant quickly contacted the client and was told that the parcel never arrived. The client's response was simple, "It was never in the contract that it had to be sent via registered post, it's not my fault it went missing".

Smelling a rat the assistant called the police; all addresses turned out to be fake and neither of the scammers have ever been found (at the time of writing).

She had lost the $3,800 that she paid the client.

Then she was charged ANOTHER $5,000 from Paypal ... Huh? ... Why would this happen as Paypal had already refunded the $5,000?!?

The credit card (that was used originally) had been stolen, but the scammers had managed to get the first refund into their own account (which they promptly closed down), but the first refund of $5,000 had been refunded to the WRONG account.

The original (stolen) credit card still wanted their $5,000 back. Even though Paypal had made a gigantic mistake there was no way that they were going to use their own money to pay for it, so they withdrew another $5,000 from the assistants account.

The assistant lost a total of $8,800.

Chapter 23 - Items damaged in the mail

I offer a refund if someone is not happy with their item. This is so they don't damage it and claim that they didn't get what they paid for.
It happens.
If a customer receives an item that they are not happy with then there is nothing stopping them from putting the item back in the box and kicking it, breaking the item. Then the item is returned with a note saying 'The item is broken, I would like a refund'. According to ebay rules they are entitled to a refund because the item wasn't as described.

Do items get broken in the mail? Yes.
I've had parcels bent that had stickers on them stating 'Please do not bend'.
My wife has received old postcards with pen stab marks in them! (How?!?)
I had a fully framed picture completely smashed; the glass had slid all over the picture during transit and made hundreds of cut marks across the picture, completely ruining it. The irony is that it had no 'fragile' or 'glass' sticker on it!

The biggest scam is when a buyer purchases your item and, when they receive it, swap the item with their own that is broken.
For example, a buyer owns a broken iPod so they buy yours. When they receive the new one they send their old one back claiming that the new one doesn't work.
The irony of this scam is that the buyer doesn't see anything wrong with doing this, claiming that it goes back to the manufacturer for repair anyway so it all evens out in the end. (Too bad if it's out of warranty).

Chapter 24 - Second chance offers

Second chance offers were big on ebay years ago. I used them myself because they were a great way of doing extra business.

Second chance offers are simple; if a person bidding on your item is unsuccessful then you may offer them the same item at the price they bid (if you have another item to sell).
For example, if I was selling a widget which person A won at $45 and Person B lost with a bid of $40 then I can offer person B another widget at $40.

Second chance offers are also used if the winning bidder withdraws from the transaction. This is very frustrating but it does happen.

Back in the old days I could send out a second chance offer and about thirty percent of buyers would buy from it; but in the last two years I have not sold anything using this method as it is now considered a scam by ebay users.

Scammers will find expensive auctions that have just finished and send *second chance offers* to all those that lost the auction. They pretend that they are the seller of the item and claim that the winning bidder has withdrawn from the transaction.
If a person decides to take advantage of this offer then they are asked to wire transfer the money so the transaction can happen quicker.
Usually scammers hurry the buyer up so it all happens too quickly, this is usually achieved by claiming that the seller is going overseas very soon.

Note that this scam can also be aimed at the winner bidder, not just the losers. This is done by the scammer emailing the winning bidder (while pretending to be the seller) and asking them to send the money via wire transfer quickly.

One scam I was made aware of was a Mountain Bike that was being sold here in Australia. When the auction finished a lady from England won it for $2,000; she had already agreed to pay for the extra shipping costs ($800).
She then received an email from a person in Turkey who claimed to be the seller; they explained that the bike was actually in Turkey and they were about to move back to Australia. She was told that if she paid quickly then the postage would be $200 in order for the bike to be sent from Turkey.
She promptly paid the scammer via wire transfer and waited for her new bike; she was very stunned when, instead, she received an email from the real seller asking where the money was. It took a few emails to work out what had really happened.

Her final email stated that she was broke so 'could he send the bike anyway?' To which the seller never replied.

50

Chapter 25 - Feedback extortion

I sell on ebay in a niche market so I have a certain type of client who I would call honest overall. In that time I've only had 2 attempts at feedback extortion.
I know some power sellers, who sell in the electronics category, that have attempts made against them *daily*!

Feedback extortion is simple; the buyer believes that you have done them wrong (or over charged, it could be any number of reasons) so they believe they should receive a few 'extras' in order for them to leave you positive feedback.
The 'extras' that the buyer refers too can be anything - from free postage, discounts or another 'cheap' item thrown in for free. Usually it's because an item is 'not quite what I expected, but if you give me another card for free I'll leave you good feedback'.

Feedback extortion is why most ebay power sellers won't leave feedback first; they will only leave it after the buyer has left it.
From personal experience - if I leave feedback for a buyer first then 80% of them will give me feedback. If I don't leave feedback first then only 30% of buyers will give me feedback.
It's to my advantage that I leave feedback first; so my new rule is simple, I only leave feedback for people who have 10 or more feedback points. Both of my extortion attempts were from people with zero feedback.

What to do? This is probably one scam where I don't have the answers. All I can do is tell you what I did in this situation.
I wrote them an email and offered them a full refund if they sent the item back - that was it. I didn't say anything about the extortion attempt or offer any other solution. In neither situation did I receive negative feedback.

All power sellers that I know simply ignore extortion attempts and accept negative feedback as a cost of running a business. They don't like it (and vent their anger on the power sellers forum board), but they don't give into it.
Remember, if you give in once they will attempt to extort you again.

Note that if the blackmailer does give you negative feedback, then proof of an extortion attempt is not reason enough for ebay to remove the feedback.
It's a rule that stinks, I know.

Chapter 26 – The Powerseller scam

The following email is like all the other scams that I have received, and the usual rules apply on how to spot it. So why does this email get it's own chapter? Because it's a scam that I have fallen victim to.

The first thing I will point out is that this email is not the exact one that I fell for, or is it an exact replica of the real powerseller email. Not many people have (or will) see what the real one looks like.
The email that I received to suck me in was the same as the real email; except at that stage I didn't know what the real one looked like!
Remember that most people only ever receive this email once; it is not often that someone is a powerseller and then gets the offer again! (Although I will be trying when I finish this book and get back to selling on ebay!)

This email is really like all the others though; it has been sent to hundreds of people ('undisclosed-recipients'), the link doesn't go to ebay (it goes to IP address of 974274610:82 – it's a nerd thing) and it doesn't have my name (or account name) anywhere.

In the last paragraph it states that _'ebay sent this email to you because you are part of the powerseller program'_ – you are not. This email is to invite you into the program and, until you accept the invitation, you are not part of the program.

Should you join? That's a personal option; but it's free and I found the powerseller forum board was worth it – and there are a lot more benefits than just the forum board.

Powerseller scam email

From: eBay
Date: 12/06/2007 03:56:37 PM
To: undisclosed-recipients:,
Subject: Congratulations! You're a PowerSeller.Get your PowerSeller benefits now

 Come Sign In!

recognized respected & rewarded

Dear eBay Member,

Congratulations on becoming a Bronze PowerSeller! You'll find that the more you use this program, the more you'll benefit. You will have access to the special services we provide and also be able to network with other successful PowerSellers.

Power Seller Important:
Congratulations! Join the eBay Bronze PowerSeller Program Now!. Come and join us. When you join the PowerSeller program, you'll be able to receive more of the support you'll need for continued success. So, why wait? Join now!

http://974274610:82/powersellers/ebay.com/index.php

The PowerSeller Portal will point the way to:

⭐ PowerSeller Priority Support via 24/7 webform.
⭐ Health care solutions information.
⭐ Exclusive offers for PowerSellers as part of your program benefits.
⭐ Free PowerSeller Business Templates.
⭐ PowerSeller discussion board.
⭐ Learn more about all of these benefits by signing in now!

Finally, please make sure you receive all PowerSeller benefits by mail, email, and telephone by opting in to accept communications from eBay. To opt in, visit the Preferences area of your My eBay page. If this is your first time as a PowerSeller, you will receive a welcome kit in the mail explaining the benefits of this program.

⚙ How do you maintain your status?
Just keep doing what you're already doing--being successful! Simply:

- Maintain the minimum average monthly sales amount for your PowerSeller level.
- Maintain a 98% positive total feedback rating.
- Maintain your account in good financial standing.
- Comply with all eBay listing and marketplace policies.
- Uphold eBay community values, including honesty, timeliness, and mutual respect.

Again, welcome to the eBay PowerSeller program!

Regards,
eBay PowerSeller Team

➦ **Go to the PowerSellers Portal**

Chapter 27 - What to do when you think you have found a fake item or account

If you know that the item (or seller) is fake then email the item number to the ebay security section and let them deal with it.

I will say the obvious here – stay away if you are unsure of the item or seller.

Remember the Golden rules when buying on ebay –
- Use your common sense
- Check out the feedback of the seller (While everyone has to start sometime, a new account is the easiest way for a scammer to work)
- Has the seller sold these sorts of items before?
- Has the account been dormant for a while? (Scammers love using accounts that the owner doesn't use anymore, this way they won't know that it's been hijacked)
- Email the seller and ask them specific questions; if you get no reply then stay away (Scammers don't spend the time answering questions unless it's for thousands of dollars)
- At the end of the day if something feels wrong then avoid the auction.

PART 3 – PAYPAL

Paypal scams are like every other scam – they rely on a person's lack of understanding on how the 'system' works. Which means your best defence is **KNOWLEDGE.**

This part of the book will teach you how Paypal works and how scams (aimed at paypal) work.

Paypal is simple. You input your credit card number into the paypal system and, when you need to transfer funds (i.e. to a seller), paypal takes the funds from your credit card and transfers it to the recipients account.
The advantage of this is that paypal is the only place that your credit card number is stored; nobody else will see the number. This reduces the amount of potential credit card fraud.

Paypal is 100% safe and has never been hacked into. All the stories you hear about paypal accounts being taken over by scammers is because of the scams that I will discuss in these next chapters.

Chapter 28 - What a scam email looks like.

All the following examples are real emails that I have received.

Example 1

Please Update Your Account

Dear valued **PayPal** member:

Due to concerns for safety, Your account has been Blocked in our system as a part of our latest security measures against Fraud and ID Theft. This happens to ensure that only you have access to your PayPal account and to ensure a safe Banking experience against online fraud. We require all Blocked accounts as yours to verify and Update their information on file with us. To Speed up the Verification and Update Process, We urge you to verify and Update your account now to avoid your online access disabled.

However, failure to update your records will result in account suspension.
Please update your records on or before Mars 20, 2007.

Once you have updated your account records, your **PayPal** session will not be interrupted and will continue as normal.

To update your **PayPal** records click on the following link:
http://www.actived-paypal.com/

PayPal, Inc.
P.O. Box 45950
Omaha, NE 68145

Sincerely,

PayPal

COMMENT: First warning sign – Paypal uses a person's real name, so the *'Dear Valued PayPal member'* means that it is fake.

Note the spelling error of the month "mars 20, 2007" – this by itself does not mean it is fake. Everyone makes mistakes; I've made a few clangers in ebay descriptions that make me go bright red when reminded of.
What you should be looking for is *Grammatical errors,* not spelling errors; most scam emails originate from Africa where English is not their first language. Any scammer can look up an English dictionary to check spelling, but it takes experience in order to use the

language properly – "*I have a concealed business suggestion for you*" is one of the more 'interesting' examples I have read.

One of the major rules that I hope you learn from this book is
DON'T CLICK ON A LINK IN AN EMAIL.
This is no exception, don't click on it – go to your web browser and type in 'www.paypal.com'; if there really is a problem then you will find out about it on the web site.

Example 2

Dear Member,

We recently noticed one or more attempts to log in to your account
from a foreign IP address.

If you recently accessed your account while traveling, the unusual log in
attempts may have been initiated by you. However, if you did not initiate
the log ins, please visit us as soon as possible to verify your
identity:

   http://maki.imagine.co.za/ATutor/users/.paypal/www.paypal.com/SecureInfo/paypal/

Verify your identity is a security measure that will ensure that you are   `http://www.paypal.com/SecureInfo/paypal/`
the only person with access to the account.

Thanks for your patience as we work together to protect your account.

Sincerely,

\-
           PROTECT YOUR PASSWORD

   NEVER give your password to anyone and ONLY log in at
https://www.paypal.com/. Protect yourself against fraudulent websites by
opening a new web browser (e.g. Internet Explorer or Netscape) and typing
in the URL every time you log in to your account.
\-

Please do not reply to this e-mail. Mail sent to this address cannot be
answered. For assistance, log in to your PayPal account and choose the
"Help" link in the header of any page.

Email ID PP321

COMMENT: This attempt was good but suffers from a major error. It actually takes you to the real paypal!
The scammer has put the fake web address in the email – 'http://maki.imagine.co.za … etc'. (Note that 'za' means that the web site is in South Africa while Paypal is in the USA) but messed up the link. It is not often that you will receive scam emails that are wrong; don't count on it happening too often.

What else have they done wrong here? I'll point the all the mistakes out.

1. It was addressed to 'Dear Member', Paypal will use your real first name when sending an email.
2. There are no company graphics or logo.
3. The 'to:' section is to *undisclosed-recipients*. When Paypal sends emails it will show your email address in that section.
4. At the bottom of the email it says 'Sincerely,' and nothing underneath. A real email will have a persons name and their title.
5. "Verify your identity is a security measure that ..." is not grammatically correct. When Paypal write a letter they are edited and anything that could cause confusion is changed.

Notice that, at the bottom of the email, it reads –

PROTECT YOUR PASSWORD

NEVER give your password to anyone and ONLY log in at https://www.paypal.com/. Protect yourself against fraudulent websites by opening a new web browser (e.g. Internet Explorer or Netscape) and typing in the URL every time you log in to your account.

This is in every paypal email and it is included here in order to make the email look authentic. This book is trying to teach exactly what this paragraph says – *type the URL into your web browser.*
The email is a fake though and is relying on you to click on the link in the email, effectively disregarding its own security advice.

Example 3

The following example is one email but has been split up into 3 sections so I can explain it easier.

This example is nearly identical to a real email that Paypal will send you when you have paid for an item using Paypal. I did check my paypal account to see if this transaction had really gone through but luckily it was just a fake.
This is a good email to teach from as it is the best example I have seen.

> *From:* PayPal
> *Date:* 03/02/2007 07:14:32 AM
> *To:* undisclosed-recipients:,
> *Subject:* You Have Paid orders@dell.com $699.99 USD using PayPal !

COMMENT: Everything is correct here except the 'To:' line. A real email from Paypal will have your real email address in that line, not 'Undisclosed-recipients'.

PayPal *The way to send and receive money online*

Dear member,

This email confirms that you have paid orders@dell.com $699.99 USD using PayPal.

This credit card transaction will appear on your bill as "PAYPAL *DELL INC".

Payment Details

Purchased From: Dell.Inc

Item #	Item Title	Quantity	Price	Subtotal
250016390196	New Dell 6400 e1505 Intel Core Duo 1.66 GHz 1GB Laptop	1	$669.95 USD	$669.95 USD

Shipping & Handling via USPS First Class Mail to 154XX (includes any seller handling fees)	$19.16 USD
Shipping Insurance (optional):	---
Sales Tax (6.000% inPA) :	$10.88 USD
Total:	$699.99 USD

Note: Thank you!

Shipping Information

Shipping Info: ▓▓▓▓▓▓▓
Brownsville, PA 15417
United States

Address Status: Confirmed▓

COMMENT: This is what an email from Paypal actually looks like. I have blacked out the 'shipping info' address in order to protect the innocent victim.

60

If it fools you then don't feel stupid. I receive about 300 of these a month (the real ones that is, not the fakes) so I know what they look like, if you only get one or two a month then you are forgiven if you are fooled.

So – how do you tell if it is a fake or not?

1. It's been sent to 'Dear Member', a real email will use my FULL name (that's first and last name).
2. The second line says 'This email confirms that you have paid …'. WRONG, it should use your name in there - 'This email confirms that you, ebayuser, have paid …'. ('ebayuser' being the username that you use on ebay.) Note that if you are using Paypal to pay for an item other than on ebay then it is slightly different again.
3. The transaction ID is missing.
4. The address is totally wrong; I'm in Australia but the shipping info is to Brownsville USA. Please note that this may be a real person who is an innocent victim here, don't send them an abusive email!

If you have questions about the shipping and tracking of your purchased item or service, please contact the seller orders@dell.com.

Do you confirm this transaction?

If this transaction was not made by you please immediately take the following steps:

- Login to your account by clicking on the link below
- Provide requested information to ensure you are the owner of the account
- Find this transaction in HISTORY and click 'Cancel Transaction'

CANCEL TRANSACTION!

Thank you for using PayPal!
The PayPal Team

http://www.climaxentertainment.com/~okada/https/www.paypal.com/cgi-bin/login.html

Please do not reply to this email. This mailbox is not monitored and you will not receive a response. For assistance, log in to your PayPal account and choose the Help link located in the top right corner of any PayPal page.

PayPal Email ID PP843

COMMENT: This is where the trouble begins!

Real emails from paypal DO NOT have the 'Do you confirm this transaction?' section, this is where the trickery begins.

This email is trying to get you to click on 'Cancel Transaction'; to do that the scammer must make you believe that your account has been hacked into and that you need to act NOW or else you will lose everything.

If you put your mouse over the 'Cancel transaction' button (BUT DO NOT CLICK IT) then, after two seconds, the web address appears. In this example I have circled the web address that appears (http://www.climaxentertainment.com/~okada ...). If you click on the 'Cancel transaction' button then you are lead to the fake web site; this will be an exact copy of the real Paypal website but it is NOT the actual Paypal site.

Example 4

```
You have added Martin.connaughton@washcoll.edu as a new e-mail address for
your PayPal account.

If you did not authorize this change or if you need assistance
with your account, please click here to contact PayPal customer service.

                        http://www.schloemmer.co.at/motobike/artmedic_event/mrtg/us/cgi-bin/index.php

Thank you for using PayPal
The PayPal Team

Please do not reply to this e-mail. Mail sent to this address cannot
be answered. For assistance, log in to your PayPal account and choose
the "Help" link in the header of any page.
```

This is a scam email I have received many of recently. When I started writing this book I had never seen one before, I now have four.

Again, they are trying to make you respond to the email. After all, wouldn't you be worried if an unknown email address was added to your paypal account?
Simply hover the mouse pointer over the words 'click here' and up comes the real web address (http://www.schloemmer.co.at/....).

Another minor error with this email is that it doesn't ask you click anywhere in order to VERIFY the new email address. If you really do add a new email address to your account then you will receive an email that asks you to verify the request – you don't have to click on this email either, just go to the web site.

This is fraud, there is no new email address on your account. If you are still worried then type in 'www.paypal.com' into your web browser and double check.

Chapter 29 - How to tell if you are at a fake Paypal web site

Fake web sites are set up to look like the real one; the only difference is what happens after you enter your details.

If you enter your details into a fake web site then you have just given those details to a scammer. More on how this works later.

To tell if you are at a fake web site there are two areas that you need to check. Firstly, check the address bar (you should always type the address in for ebay, paypal and your financial institute).

If it says anything other than www.paypal.com (for paypal) then you are looking at a fake web.

The screenshot above shows the address bar in Internet Explorer (IE), IE is the most common web browser.

Note that there should not be ANYTHING before the 'https:' and NOTHING after the '.com'.

If you have looked carefully you may notice that most web sites have 'http://' in front of them while this one starts with 'https://'; this is normal as the extra 's' stands for 'security'.

If you are interested - 'http' stands for *Hyper Text Transfer Protocol* while 'https' stands for *Hyper Text Transfer Protocol Security*.

In the above screenshot there is a padlock at the bottom right corner (which I have put a circle around) to show that this is a secure site.
Paypal is a secure site and if you can't see this padlock (it usually appears in the bottom right corner) then it's a fake web site.

The screenshot below is from the program 'Opera' (a competitor of Internet Explorer).
As you can see, www.paypal.com appears in the address bar (correct) and the padlock appears (inside the circle); the only difference here is that the padlock is at the right end of the address bar – this is fine, as long as it appears!

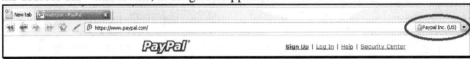

Chapter 30 - How the scam works

When you are on the fake web site you will be asked to enter your details, as the screenshot below shows.

If it is a fake web site then your details are sent to the scammer without you realising.

Now that you have 'logged in' you are taken to another page that explains your account is under suspension and, now that you have verified your identity, will be re-activated within 24 hours. You are also asked not to access your account in these 24 hours or the computer will re-suspend your account.

This is all a scam to get you to not use your account for 24 hours while the scammers have your account details. In this time the scammer will log into your real paypal account and transfer all your funds to their own account; remember that most paypal accounts are linked to your credit card so that's a lot of money that can be stolen.

In those 24 hours they will also remove all traces to themselves.

Some notes to remember about how paypal works –
- An account is not verified by e-mail, they will ring you
- When an account is verified it is immediately re-activated; it does not take 24 hours.
- If your account has been suspended for any reason then ring paypal, paypal are very good at security and will discuss anything over the phone (you will have to verify your own identity first though!).
- There is NO reason why paypal will ever block access to your own account; they may freeze your funds so you can't use it but they won't block access.
- Paypal's computer will not re-suspend you simply for accessing your own account, it simply doesn't work that way.

Chapter 31 – What to do if you receive a suspicious email

When I receive a scam email that involves Paypal I send a copy to spoof@paypal.com (if the email involves ebay then I send a copy to spoof@ebay.com), this way they have a copy and can take action to shut down the scammers illegal web site.
Please note that if you receive a scam email please forward it onto the email addresses I have specified and then delete it.

When you do send an email to paypal (or ebay) they will reply (not a personal reply though) verifying that it is a scam and what to do if you have given your account details to the scammers.

Below is a copy and paste of the email that paypal sends; please note that this email is copyright of paypal and no infringement is intended.

Dear James,

Thank you for taking the time to contact spoof@paypal.com. The email you reported was not sent by PayPal and is a phishing (fraudulent) email.

What to do Next

Delete the phishing email. If you've already responded to the email, please log in to your PayPal account and perform some important safety measures.

1. Go to your Profile and change your password and security questions.

2. Review the payments listed on your Account Overview.

If you notice a payment that you don't recognize, visit the PayPal Security Center to file a claim. We'll promptly investigate any suspicious transactions and you won't be held liable for unauthorized payments sent from your account.

Visit the PayPal Security Center

In the new PayPal Security Center you'll find fraud-fighting tips, tools, and technology.

You'll learn:
* Ways to stay safe online
* How to spot fake emails
* What to do if you suspect unauthorized activity in your account

You'll also find tools to help protect against identity theft:
* Equifax credit alerts: Receive notifications about activity on your credit accounts
* eBay Toolbar: Download a toolbar that warns you when you□re on a potentially fraudulent web site

```
------------------------------------
Safeguard Your Account
------------------------------------
```
Phishing emails often try to get your attention by telling you that there's a problem with your account.

One way to figure out if an email is really from PayPal is to open a new browser and log in to your PayPal account. Any important information about your account will be displayed once you are logged in.

```
------------
Thank You
------------
```
By alerting us to this phishing email, you're taking an active role in keeping the PayPal community safe. Users like you are our greatest partners in combating spoof.

We'll use the information you provided to work with law enforcement to shut down the fraudulent website.

Sincerely,
 PayPal

```
******************************************************************************
```
Remember, PayPal will never ask you for your password in an e-mail.
There are no exceptions to this policy. If someone claiming to be from PayPal asks you for your password in response to an e-mail, you should refuse to provide it and contact us. To contact PayPal, go to the PayPal Help Center and click the "Contact Us" link.

COMMENT: In the last paragraph it states that *"Remember, PayPal will never ask you for your password in an e-mail."* I have explained that point a lot in this book, and here PayPal writes it!

At the bottom they ask you to contact PayPal by going to the paypal website, through the help centre, and clicking on the "contact us" link – that's the best way of doing it, don't click on an email.
Note that there is no link to click in this email!

PayPal do spend a lot of time and money on security. They have been successful in shutting down fraudulent websites quickly so please don't be afraid to use PayPal for international transactions (I do!).

Chapter 32 - The truth about Paypal's own protection policy

Paypal is a helpful company but have become a victim of their own success.

Make no mistake - Paypal is the single best way to send money around the world; unfortunately, because of the amount of money and the ease of use, criminals are drawn to it because they see it as an easy target.

For a scammer to rob a bank they must circumvent the bank's security system; to rob a paypal member all they need to do is rely on the customers lack of knowledge (or lack of experience). With over 100 million members scammers will always find a target; a scammer once admitted that 1 in 30,000 people respond to a scam email.

As scammers refine their techniques though, more and more members will be tricked into giving away their own confidential information.

So what to do if you have been scammed? According to Paypal's policy they will refund the lost amount.

This policy has resulted in a lot of money lost by Paypal in refunds; now the policy has been revised so only the amount that they can recoup from the scammers account is refunded. If the scammer takes the funds out of their own account before Paypal can recoup any of your money then you will not be reimbursed.

This is why scammers don't want you to access your account for 24 hours, because if you do then you will complain and get the funds reimbursed. By convincing you not to access your account for 24 hours this gives them time to take the money out of the system so you can't get it back.

Lets recap that because it is important – Paypal will only refund the stolen money if they can get it back from the scammers account; if the scammer has taken the money out of their own account before you lodge a complaint then you will receive nothing.

If Paypal has taken money out of your credit card then you may ring your credit card company and have the transaction reversed.

If you do this then Paypal will demand the funds be repaid before you can use the account again.

So choose carefully; if you get the credit card company to refund your money then you won't be able to use your paypal account again. This is a choice that you need to think seriously about before you take any action.

PART 4 – OTHER INTERNET SCAMS

So far I have concentrated on showing scams that target ebay and Paypal users, but they are far from being the only scams that are perpetrated on a daily basis.

The following are several scams that have been going on for years.
I have used the Internet since 1996 and the Nigerian letter scam was going on back then.

Chapter 33 - Banks

In Australia we have several leading banking establishments, all of who are all targeted by scammers.

I personally bank with two different banks (one is my personal account and the other is business) and I never receive real emails from either of them (I receive some annoying phone calls offering me insurance but that's another matter).

About every two to three days I will receive an email that purports to be from my bank.

First question you will probably ask when you receive one of these emails is – how do they know which bank I'm with?
The answer is simple – they don't. What they do is send out false emails for all the banks and hope that the person who receives the email is a member of that bank.
Over the past year I have received over twenty scam emails from each of the major banks in Australia, in that same period I have received over 100 fake emails from foreign banks – banks that I didn't even know existed, let alone bank with.

Example 1

Westpac

WESTPAC BANK SECURITY

Accessing your Westpac online banking from another country or from another computer I freezed.

We have taken this action because your Westpac bank online account may have been c respond to tropans,worms and and effected virus files and it allows fraudulate activities investigative procedures that led to this conclusion, Please note that we took this action

To complete our activation process for your account restoring access,please click here:
https://online.westpac.com.au/esis/Login/S...

Regards. http://www.buffyangelguild.com/poll1/php/Westpac/Westpac/

Westpac Bank Security Department.

Accounts Management As outlined in our User Agreement, Westpac Bank® will periodically send you inforn

Visit our Privacy Policy and User Agreement if you have any questions.
Westpac Bank Security and Privacy

COMMENT: Westpac is an Australian bank that I don't use, but I do know that the logo used here is correct. This is not surprising as the logo appears all over the Westpac web site and other advertising material.

The objective of this email, and all other fake emails from financial institutes, is to get you to click on the email. So remember the Golden rule - **NEVER CLICK ON A LINK IN AN EMAIL**.
If you think it might be real then go to the bank's web site by typing in the web address, not by clicking on the link provided. If you are still unsure then ring your bank.
If the email states that you must respond to the email, and only that way, then the email is fake.

A trick to working out if a link is real or not is to hold the mouse pointer over the link WITHOUT clicking on it. After a second the real web address will appear, in the example above I have put a circle around the real link.

Example 2

COMMENT: The real website this will take you to is 'ilpkl.gov.my', not the ANZ web site.

Example 3

Capital One | what's in your wallet?

We have been notified that a card associated with your account has been reported
have temporarely limited access to sensitive Capital One Online Banking account f

To ensure that your account is not compromised please take a review on your rece
deposits, and check your account profile to make sure no changes have been mad
account, report this to Capital One Security Center immediately.

To get started, please click the link below:

https://service.capitalone.com/oas/login.do?objectclicked=LoginSplash

b://rds.yahoo.com/_ylt=A0oGkkc89eREaekARGxXNyoA;_ylu=X3oDMTB2cXVjNTM5BGNvbG8Ddv
Online Banking and its service providers are committed to protecting your privacy a
through e-mail.

You can view our privacy policy and contact information at
http://www.capitalone.com/protection/privacy/index.php

COMMENT: 'Capital one'? Never heard of them. As I said before, scammers send
scam emails to everyone in the hope that at least one person gets sucked in.

Example 4

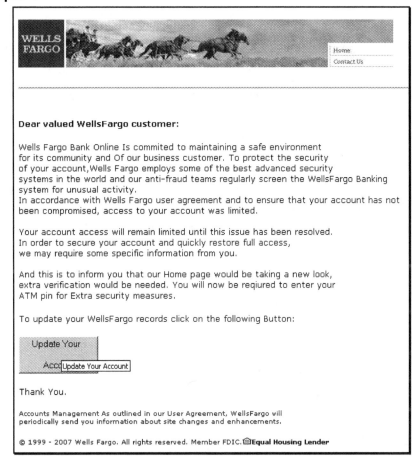

COMMENT: Big problem here as the link has been replaced by a button. I have placed my mouse pointer over the button but it only displays 'Update your Account' not the website of your destination.

Just because there is a button in the email does not mean it's legitimate. You need to remember the other rules I hope you have learnt from this book, and that is to go into the 'WellsFargo' web site by typing the web address into your Internet browser – do not click on the button.
If you are still confused then ring your financial institute.

Further examples

Here is a small selection of other scam emails, targeting financial institutes, that I have received. All are **fake** by the way.

Bank of America — Online Banking

Dear Valued Customer,
- Our new security system will help you to avoid frequently fraud transactions and to keep your deposited funds in safety.
- Due to technical update we recommend you to reactivate your account.

Click on the link below to login and begin using your updated Bank of America account.
To log into your account, please visit the Bank of America website at:

http://www.bankofamerica.com/update-account/index.jsp

Bank of America — **Higher Standards**
Military Bank

Dear Bank Of America Military Bank member,

During our regularly scheduled account maintenance and verification procedures, we have detected a slight error in your account information. This may be a direct result of fraudulent online activity, or identity theft. Please click the link below and login into your account on our secure web site and follow the steps to verify your data.

Click here to begin.

This is  http://wendylaw.com/text/.https://bankofamerica.militarybankonline.com/efs/servlet/military/login.htm

Dear Regions Bank valued customer,

This is the official notification from Regions Bank. We are sorry to inform you that your online
services are expired, and must be reactivated immediately, if you intend to use this services in the
future, and prevent any similarly situations you must take action at once!

Click the link below and reactivate your Online Banking account.

http://www.regions.com/cgi-forte/forteisapi.dll?ServiceName=update&

http://www.camaradirecta.com/help/users/EB/logon/user.htm

Thank you for the privilege of serving you.

Sincerely,

John Peck,
President and CEO

Bank of America   Online Banking

> Online Banking Alert

Remember:
Always look for
your SiteKey before
you enter your
passcode during
Sign In »

Security Update Notification

Dear Valued Customer :

Sign in to Bank of America Online Banking.

We are unable to activate your account because we have just upgraded our online security parameters to make yo[u]
secured from online frauds,so we request that you reconfirm your online Banking details with the one we have on f[ile]
receive money online.

Your account may be place on restricted status. Restricted accounts continue to receive payments, but they are lim[ited]
funds. To lift this restriction, you need to login into your account (with your username or SSN and your password), t[o]
process. You must reconfirm your credit card details and your billing information as well. All restricted accounts ha[ve]
meaning that you may no longer send money from your account until you have reconfirm your billing information o[n]

Click here to Sign in to Online Banking to reactivate your Bank account now.

Thank You.

Because your reply will not be transmitted via secure e-mail, the e-mail address that generated this alert will not a[...]
Bank of America with questions or comments, please **sign in to Online Banking** and visit the customer service sectio[n]

Chapter 34 - Nigerian letter scam

The *Nigerian Letter scam* is Nigeria's fourth biggest 'export' (after Oil, Cocoa and Rubber). The country depends on the revenue that these scammers bring in.

Please note that this scam is also known as the '419' scam in the USA ('419' is the fraud section in the Nigerian penal code).

Nigeria has one of the highest corruption rates in the world; what makes it even worse is that they have vast quantities of oil that are exported every year. According to the CIA 80% of oil revenue goes to a 'select' few government officials.
This makes for a lot of 'lost' funds. (One official was reported to have six hundred million dollars in a Swiss bank account.)

Other countries I have seen used in this scam include Ethiopia, Libya, Sierra Leone and Ivory-Lana. The stupid thing here is that 'Ivory-Lana' isn't a real country - it's in the 'Phantom: Ghost who walks' comic book. (The country I think they meant is 'Ivory Coast'.)
The one thing all these countries have in common is that they have massive oil reserves (I don't know about Ivory-Lana though, the comic book never specified that).

These scams will convince you that you are simply transferring funds out of their country and into your bank account; for which you will receive twenty percent of the funds as payment (this could equate to a hundred million dollars depending on the email).
You believe that you are scamming the country when in fact you are being scammed; you will NEVER see any money, you will in fact be paying money to the scammers for a variety of reasons.

So why don't these people get caught? Firstly, someone needs to lodge a complaint; how many people are prepared to complain about a scammer while admitting that they were knowingly trying to defraud a foreign government of millions of dollars? And make no mistake about it, you are trying to defraud a foreign government.

This scam started in the 1950's via (snail) mail. The scammers would get names and addresses from magazines and newspapers, so the victim would receive the letter personally addressed to them; this lead to people believing that the letter was real.
The only thing that hampered this scam was the fact that a lot of time and money was needed, the scammers needed to pay for the envelopes, paper and other items. At the start the scammers paid for their stamps (they quickly learnt how to forge these so it ceased being an expense) so it was costing the scammer about a dollar for each letter that they sent.

Even today letters are sent out; the US mail system claims to have burnt four tonnes of Nigerian scam letters in one day because of forged stamps.

The Internet changed everything.

No longer do the scammers need to learn the name of their targets, and they certainly don't need to pay for all the email that they send.

To send email is free, the cost is no different if you send out one hundred or one hundred million in a day.

Currently there are no email filters to stop email from a particular country, the only defence we have at this time is spam filters that try to stop the individual emails. With the amount of money that can be made by scammers it is a constant battle between them and spam filters; you will always receive scam emails. I personally receive about ten a week even with a powerful spam filter active on my account (without the filter it is around one hundred per day).

I have read an article that claimed people in the Australian state of Queensland (home to three million people) lose two million dollars a week to this scam; so don't think it is a small problem.

I have personally never been involved in this scam but I have read hundreds of emails from victims. They ask me if they are involved in a scam, to which I've got the unenviable job of telling them that they are.

I also have to explain that they have lost everything that they have already sent the scammers; sometimes this runs into the tens of thousands of dollars.

As I do the final edits of this book I have come across a new method of how you are contacted – online dating sites.

If you put your profile up on these sites then you will be contacted by an African female that wants to marry you if only you will help her transfer her money first. This amount is usually three to eight million dollars (Euros is the most common currency specified). The money is usually her inheritance.

How it works

The first trick the scammers will use is to get in conversation with you. This is usually achieved by explaining what they want, but they do have other methods. I will admit that some of their methods confuse even me.

As they refine their techniques they learn what works and what doesn't. This means that they will only improve.

The following is an example of the most common Nigerian scam. Please note that all the examples that I use have not been changed except the web site links have been deleted.

Example 1

Sir/Madam Kindly allow me the modesty of introducing myself.

I am Mariam Bobbi the daughter of the former head of state president of Congo-Kinshasha (former Zaire) Mr.Laurent Desire Kabila. I got your particulars through the South African Chamber of Commerce; However, I am contacting you in order to ask for your assistance on this confidential Business proposal with full financial benefit for both of us.
Before I go into further details, please be informed that I am writing without any other person(s) pre-knowledge of my contacting you on this transaction. Therefore I will appreciate same attitude to be maintained all through. I have the sum of USD8.5 Million from a secret
Sale of Diamond by my father before he was assassinated by one of his body Guard (Rashid) on January 16th 2001, which I will like you to receive on my Behalf due to security reasons, as my narration below will explain. But before I continue be well informed that your share in this transaction has been calculated at 30% of the total sum of USD$8.5M, 5% for expenses and the rest for my Family and me.

My father as a real African traditionalist was a polygamist thereby having married so many wives, and my mother being the second wife of my father, my stepbrother Joseph, who is the current president of my country, is the son of the first wife and he does not have any knowledge about this deal.

Already president Joseph is using his power to colonize all the money and private property, which my father left behind for the whole family. Now my mother and I are left with nothing in the inheritance of my late father's wealth. Our situation is seriously critical that we need your assistance to help us receive these funds overseas for proper investment. Let me quickly assure you the 100% safe proof of this transaction because the diamond sales are packaged from the onset in a pattern that shows no direct trace or linkage with us (Kabila family). At present the money is in cash and is secured in a security company as family

Treasures, as I don't want to deposit the money in a financial institution for fear of the funds being confiscated the consignment will be released within seven (7) days of my being in receipt of your reply.

Via my email address above only for security reasons. I am waiting for your swift and favourable response, and in case you have any question(s), do not hesitate to contact me through my email
Best Regards,

Ms Mariam Bobbi

COMMENT: Does it sound good? Read Wikipedia and you can verify all the information (Joseph Kabila is the current President, Mr. Laurent Desire Kabila was his father and was also (stepbrother) Joseph's father).

In fact the Wikipedia entry even has the same spelling mistakes that are made in crucial areas of this letter. This shows that Wikipedia is where all the scammers do their 'research'.

All these letters are the same in the following areas –

- They know you will be surprised that they have contacted you, but they have heard that you are a reliable person.
- They got your contact details from a reliable source (In the example above it was the *South African Chamber of Commerce*). Some emails claim that god gave them your email address.
- They are related to a corrupt official who is now dead.
- They need money transferred NOW, and it will be in the millions.
- They are willing to offer you 20% - 40% for your help.
- All you need to do is allow them to transfer the money into your bank account, that's all, nothing more – and they really do mean nothing; you just sit back and relax while they do all the work.
- 95% of the time the email is from a Hotmail or Yahoo address; this allows them to be anonymous.
- They can't transfer the money themselves.
- They claim that the 'system' in their country won't allow them to do some things that could be easily done in other countries – like transfer funds, or fly out of the country with a diamond in your handbag.
- If you get further involved you will realise that the money needs to be transferred to other countries before it can get to your account (in my case Australia). Why does the money have to go from Congo -> South Africa -> Netherlands -> England -> Australia?

Let's get one thing perfectly clear, you are being asked to help defraud the government (whether you agree with the current government or not makes no difference).
The irony of the situation is that you will end up being defrauded.

Before I explain the scam I will show a few more examples –

Example 2

Dear

I am Mr Joe Ukpoma I need your services in a confidential matter regarding money transfer.

This requires a private arrangement though the details of the transaction will be furnish to you if you indicate your interest in this proposal.

We have all the legal documents to back up the transaction, besides we have worked out the modalities to ensure smooth and risky free transfer.

We are willing to offer you 40% of the money, the fund in question is quite large. All correspondences will be via email and telephone for now.

I am expecting to hear from you, if you are willing to do the business with us,your private phone number is needed.

Please let me hear from you immediately only in my private email box: : joe_desk@excite.com

Waiting to hear from you.

Thanks,
Yours Faithfully,
Mr. Joe Ukpoma

Example 3

Attention: ,

I have a transaction of mutual benefits, which I like to share with you. For individual or group of people who desires to set up an investment firm or are in need of investment funding to boost the production of their goods, services to the end users and in returns make further profit. We have good news for you and this might interest you.

For proper availability of investment funding and support to achieve your vision and your company fully set up or financed our organization will assist you to bring this to reality as you get good yield of money in your investment.

A consult with an investor to invest the sum of 35Million Dollars in partnership with you of which commission in % will be paid to you, me for successful getting of this fund to you and investment of the fund with you in all profit made.

If you are interested, please reply instantly and forward your telephone number so we can discuss and I shall provide you with the details of providing investment funding to aid your vision.

Reply to my personal email address: chelsea_collinsa1@hotmail.co.uk

Thank you.
MR. CHELSEA COLLINS

Example 4

Dear Sir/ Madam,

Let me start by introducing myself. I am Mr. Patrick Haul credit
officer of Standard Bank Ltd South Afirca.I have a concealed business
suggestion for you.
Before the U.S and Iraqi war our client Mr Ahmed Sule who was an Iraqi
BusinessMan and also Deals On Arms With The South African Government
made a numbered fixed deposit for 18 calendar months, with a value of
Fourteen million Five Hundred Thousand United State Dollars only in my
branch. Upon maturity several notices were sent to him,even during the
war, again after the war several notifications were sent and still no
response came from him. We later found out that the Mr Sule and his family
had been killed during the war in a bomb blast that hit their home in
Iraq.
After further investigation it was also discovered that Mr Sule did not
declare any next of kin in his official papers
including the paper work of his bank deposit. And he also confided in
me the last time he was at my office that no one except me knew of his
deposit in my bank. So, Fourteen million Five Hundred Thousand United
State Dollars is still lying in my bank and no one will ever come forward
to claim it. What bothers me most is that according to the laws of my
country at the expiration three years the funds will revert to the
ownership of the South African Government if nobody applies to claim the
funds.

Against this backdrop, my suggestion to you is that I will like you as
a foreigner to stand as the next of kin to Mr Ahmed Sule so that you
will be able to receive his funds.

WHAT IS TO BE DONE:
I want you to know that I have had everything planned out so that we
shall come out successful. I have contacted an attorney that will prepare
the necessary document that will back you up as the next of kin to Mr
Ahmed Sule,all that is required from you at this stage is for you to
provide me with your full Names and Address so that the attorney can
commence his job.

After you have been made the next of kin, the attorney will also fill
in for claims on your behalf and secure the necessary approval and
letter of probate/Administration in your favor for the movement of the funds
to an account that will be provided by you.

There is no risk involved at all in the matter as we are going adopt a
legalized method and the attorney will prepare all the necessary
documents.

Please endeavor to observe utmost discretion in all matters concerning
this issue.Once the funds have been transferred to your nominated bank
account we shall share in the ratio of 65% for me, 30% for you and 5%
for any expenses incurred during the course of this operation.

Should you be interested please send me your private phone and fax
numbers for easy communication, you can write me via my private box and i
will provide you with more details of this operation.
Your earliest response to this letter will be appreciated.

please get back to me via my peasonal email: patrickhaul001@yahoo.com
to be attended to quickly

Regards.

Patrick Haul

Example 5

From Rose Guei.
Abidjan cote D`Ivoire
West Africa.

Dearest One,

I am the first duaghter of an ex military/ex president been an opposition party to the
present Government of COTE D`IVOIRE. On the 19th sept 2002 my father/mother
including every members of our family was murdered by the unknown REBELS during the
time they attack our house by shooting and looting, even this is one of the things that
contributed to the present crisis in our country today.

God so kind I was not in town when the incident
occurred, the plans of the REBELS is to kill every members of our family so that no one
will rise up to revenge as time goes on. I am in our country without any one knowing
although I am on hiding so that the unknown REBELS will not get to me and kill me like
they killed all the members of our family.

 Why I still stay back in our country is to transfer the $18.5mUSD which my late father
deposited in the custody of one of the SECURITY ASSISTANCE COMPANY,here in
Abidjan,he deposited the fund as a family treasure containing AFRICAN ART WORK FOR
EXPORT for security reasons, as security company does not operate as bank where
some one can deposit his/her money openly.

Before the death of my father he gave me the covering
documents of the fund deposited in the security company, as I am his first duaghter and
he so much loved me that was why he made me the beneficiary of the two iron trunk
boxes containing the $18.5mUSD.
Right now I wish to transfer this fund to you so that you will assist me to invest the money
into any viable sector in your country, also you will help me to join you in your country for
me to start up a new life with you there immediately the fund gets to you. since I am no

longer safe as far as Africa is concern at the moment, I wanted to transfer the fund before leaving the country because this fund is my last hope and the only hope I have now.

Before I even pick you to assist me I have prayed and slept over it asking God to provide for me a Godly minded person that will assist me in this transaction.
I will give you more details of the transaction in my next mail.
Awaiting to here from you.

Thanks and God bless you.

Rose Guei.

Example 6

Hello Dear,

It is my great pleasur to contact you in this feasible & realistic
business transaction.My name is Mr.David Mark, and I work in the
International Operation Department in a Bank here in London.I feel quite
safe dealing with you in this important business.Though, this medium
(Internet) has been greatly abused, I choose to reach you through it
because it still remains the fastest medium of communication. However,
this correspondence is unofficial and private, and it should be treated
as such.

At first I will like to assure you that this transaction is 100% risk
and trouble free to both parties. WE WANT TO TRANSFER OUT MONEY FROM OUR
BANK HERE IN LONDON. THE FUND FOR TRANSFER IS OF CLEAN ORIGIN. THE OWNER
OF THIS ACCOUNT IS A FOREIGNER, a program leader.Until his death,The
Late Prime Minister, Mr. Rafik Hariri, has a huge investment here in the
United Kingdom and all over the world, as a matter of fact he has the
sum of (THIRTY SIX MILLION SEVEN HUNDRED AND FIFTY NINE THOUSAND POUNDS
STERLINGS) in his account here in London which he deposited as a family
valuables.The family do not know about this deposit.I was on a routine
inspection that I discovered a dormant domiciliary account with a BAL.
Of (THIRTY SIX MILLION SEVEN HUNDRED AND FIFTY NINE THOUSAND POUNDS
STERLINGS) on further discreet investigation, I also discovered that the
account holder has passed away (dead) leaving no beneficiary to the
account. The bank will approve this money to any foreigner because the
former operator of the a/c is a foreigner. I am certainly sure that
nobody will come again for the claim of this money. A foreigner can
only claim this money with legal claims to the account Holder,

Therefore I need your cooperation in this transaction. I will provide
all necessary information needed in order to claim this money.Hoping in
God that you will never let me down now and in future.o.k! Rafik Bahaa
Edine Hariri (November 1, 1944 - February 14, 2005), married to Nazek
Audi Hariri, was a Lebanese self-made billionaire and business tycoon,
and was five times Prime Minister of Lebanon (1992-1998 and 2000-2004)
before his last resignation from office on October 20, 2004. The late

Rafik Hariri died on February 14, 2005 when explosives equivalent to
around 300 kg of C4 were detonated as his motorcade drove past the
Saint George Hotel i n the Lebanese capital, for more information
please log on to (***Link deleted as the web site was fabricated in order back up the claims
made in this email ***)

I WANT TO TRANSFER THIS MONEY INTO A SAFE FOREIGN ACCOUNT ABROAD
BUT I
DON'T KNOW ANY FOREIGNER WHOM I CAN TRUST, I KNOW THAT THIS
MESSAGE WILL
COME TO YOU AS A SURPRISE AS WE DON'T KNOW OURSELVES BEFORE, BUT
BE SURE
THAT IT IS REAL AND A GENUINE BUSINESS. I CONTACT YOU BELIEVING THAT
YOU
WILL NOT LET ME DOWN ONCE THE FUND GOES INTO YOUR ACCOUNT. Let me
hear
from you urgently through this Email <davmarkpin01@rediffmail.com>

Best Regards,

Mr.David Mark.

COMMENT: That's enough examples for the run of the mill Nigerian scam; hopefully
you now have a felling of what they look like. Remember, no matter how legitimate it
looks they are all LIES!!

The next set of examples show other ways that the scammers try to engage you in
conversation from which they will then set up the scam.

Example 7

EQUIP Consultants:Private Investigators and Security Consultants is conducting a
standard process investigation on behalf of Citi Bank the international Banking
conglomerate, and we will like you to assist with this Independent Enquiry.

My name is Eric Keith. I am a senior partner in the firm. This investigation involves a client
who shares the same surname with you and also the circumstances surrounding
investments made by this client at Citi Bank The Citi Bank Banking client died intestate
and nominated no successor in title over the investments made with the Bank. The
essence of this communication with you is to request you provide us
information/comments on any or all of the four issues:

1-Are you aware of any relative/relation who shares your same surname

2-Are you aware of any investment of considerable value made by such a person at the
Citi Bank?

3-Born on the 1st of June 1927

84

4-Can you establish beyond reasonable doubt your eligibility to assume status of successor in title to the deceased?

It is pertinent that you inform us ASAP whether or not you are familiar with this personality that we may put an end to this communication with you and our inquiries surrounding this personality. You must appreciate that we are constrained from providing you with more detailed information at this point.

Please respond to this mail as soon as possible to afford us the opportunity to close this investigation. Thank you for accommodating our enquiry.Please reply through this emailaddress (equip2consultants@yahoo.com.hk)

Eric Keith.

For: Equip Consultants.

COMMENT: I got a quick question for you Eric – what's my Surname if it's that important? And why is your email address a Yahoo one?

Note that if you answer 'yes' to any of Eric's four questions then he'll find a way to have the money transferred to your account after fudging the paperwork; for a fee of course.

Example 8

Dear Friend,
I am very happy to inform you about my success in getting
that fund Transfer,I want you to contact my secretary on the
information below.
NAME;(chukwuike)
Get in
touch with him on how to send you the total sum of
($1,300,000.00usd) one million,three hundred us dollars,
which I kept for your compensation.
Contact him on this email:(
chukwuike_2001@yahoo.fr)
Regards,
Dr.Hill ifeanyicjim

COMMENT: This scam is like all the others, it is trying to engage you in conversation. This is achieved by, hopefully, getting you to answer the email to say that the email has been sent to the wrong person.

Also, note that none of the scammers use their own name. In this case if you pronounce the persons last name in this example you'll see that they believe the whole thing is funny – "Dr Hill *I've been Victim*".

Example 9

my dear friend

How are you today?

It's has been long I heard from you. Well, I just want to use this medium to thank you very much foryour earlier assistance to help me in receiving the funds,without any positive out come.Iam obliged to inform you that I have succeeded in receiving the funds with the help of a new partner from Paraguay.Everythng was perfectly done because we strike a deal with one of the ladyaccountant who works with the federal Ministry of Finance (FMF) and she rendered a tremendous help to us.My new partner initiated this idea and everything worked outsuccessfully.In appreciation of your earlierassistance to me in receiving the Funds.

I have decided to compensate you with the sum of in a Cashier's$850,000 cheque (Eight Hundred andFifty ThousandUnited States Dollars).This is from my own share. I did this simply to show you that it is good to do goodthings to the right people always.Presently, I am in Paraguay for investment project with my own share under the advice of my partner.Meanwhile, I didn't forget your past efforts and attempts to assist me in transferring those fund despite thatit failed us somehow. I will be sending you e-mail from time to time to know if you haver received your share or not.Now contact my personal assistantin Benin Mr Bough Johnson , his e-mail address is (boughjohnson20@yahoo.dk)

Please do let me know immediately if you receive it so that we can share thejoy together after all the suffering at that time. In the moment, I am very busy here in Paraguay because of the investment projects, which the new partnerand I are having at hand so fill free to get in touch with young Johnson to send the cheque toyou without any delay.
With My Best Regards,
Barrister Ben ,

COMMENT: Hopefully you get the general idea.

At this stage they are only trying to get you into conversation. If you reply then you will be told more 'facts' which sound very plausible. It all sounds true because of the scammers experience from previous attempts, not because it is factual. This experience has been gained from thousands of previous scams that they have run, whether the scam was successful or unsuccessful the scammers still learn.

The reason the scammers wish to send the money to you is so they can move to your country; this way, when they arrive, their money is ready and waiting for them (courtesy of your bank account).

How you get scammed

Please note that in this example I will be using the word 'you' as the potential victim; this is done only for the reason that it is easier for me to write it.
This article has been written from real emails and conversation logs that I have been sent from victims; this example is a combination of several victims (all names withheld).

The first thing the scammers will convince you is how easy it will all be; in fact, all you need to do is send them your bank details and then sit back and wait; the money will be transferred within seven days and you can have your share straight away.
In this example the scammer wishes to transfer twenty five million dollars, and your share will be two million dollars (amounts vary wildly from one scam to the next).

For this example lets just say that you agreed to transfer the money.

Now the scammers want to pull out because they don't know if they can trust you.
After some thought the scammers decide that you need to send the scammers some money as a deposit; after all – how do they know you won't simply take their money and disappear? (The irony!)
By this stage you have been hooked; you believe (or want to believe) that the money is sitting there waiting for you. So you send them a deposit (I have heard of amounts of around five thousand dollars).
The scammers tell you that this deposit will be used for them to fly over after the transfer is complete. (Remember that the scammers wish to move to your country after the transaction is complete – don't worry though, no transaction ever gets completed!)

You pay the deposit and wait for the transfer to occur.

Uh-oh! Small problem. A bank official doesn't believe that this is a legitimate transaction so he has held up the funds!
This official is only earning one hundred and fifty dollars a week so if you bribed him three thousand dollars then he will release the funds.

By this time you will be talking to the scammers via Internet Chat –
    Scammer – We need $3000 to bribe the official.
    You – Why do you need me to pay it? Can't you take it out of the funds?
    Scammer – None of the funds are being released; we have no money to pay for this ourselves.
    You – Pay it out of the deposit I gave you, there should be enough.

Scammer – That money has already been used to buy our plane tickets, please don't allow us to come to your country with no money – we need you to get this money for us, please.

You – I can't afford another $3000; I already borrowed as much as I could to get the original $5000.

Scammer – Why are you worried about borrowing $3000 when you are about to receive $2 million?

You – I can't afford the $3000!

Scammer – You are about to become a multi millionaire! How can you have problems getting $3000? Borrow it from someone, anyone, tell them that you will give them $6000 next week.

You – I don't know about this.

Scammer – Why are you worried? The money is there, waiting for you. All we need to do is bribe the official that can transfer the money, what can go wrong?

You – Okay.

So you borrow the money from your parents, you don't want to tell them that you are involved in defrauding a foreign government so you tell them that you need the money to pay for a deposit for a car.

Are you really lying? You'll be buying a new car next week anyway with your two million dollars, and you'll be able to repay your parents with interest!

The scammers contact you and tell you that the money has been successfully transferred to South Africa. …. Huh? … why the heck has the money been transferred to South Africa?!?

So you ask why the money has been transferred to South Africa. The scammers reply that foreign transactions originating from Nigeria need to be approved by the Central Bank unless they are going to South Africa.

You are told that there is nothing to worry about and now that the money is out of Nigeria nothing can stop it.

Another problem has occurred – an official in the South African bank has told the Nigerian authorities about the transaction. This Nigerian official demands an eight thousand dollar bribe.

You are asked to pay the eight thousand.

Again you protest, again the scammers ask you why you are complaining about such a little amount of money when you will be getting millions of dollars from this transaction?

You plead that you can't get the money and that you have borrowed all the money that you can. The scammers agree that you have been good for them so they agree to increase your share up to THREE million dollars to compensate you for your extra help!

Three million dollars changes everything. You decide to 'borrow' the money from your work; after all, you will be giving the money back within five days.

So you pay the bribe, you have now given them sixteen thousand dollars.

88

Now you are told that the South African bank is charging a *customs charge* on transfers over a million dollars. The charge is twelve thousand dollars and you need to pay it.

You ask why they can't take the twelve thousand dollars out of the twenty five million dollars that is being transferred?

The scammers scold you for being so pedantic and arguing over fees that are normal business practice in their country. They explain that the banking system in Nigeria (and South Africa) works differently to the Australian system; it's not worse, only different.

You apologise for questioning their methods, and you actually feel bad that you even thought they were trying to scam you. (These scammers are very good at what they do.)

You believe that this is the final bribe as it is a tax that is charged by the South African government and that the funds are ready to be transferred.

So you convince your wife that you have cancer and you will need to borrow against the house to pay for treatment (a victim really did this).

You borrow the twelve thousand from the bank, using your house as collateral, which is promptly paid to the scammers. You have now given the scammers twenty eight thousand dollars.

Now another official wants a bribe ... the money has been transferred to Amsterdam, need to pay fees to the Amsterdam bank ... the money has accidentally been transferred back to South Africa, need another bribe ... one of the scammers has gone to hospital, you need to send them money to pay costs or else they can't sign the papers ... the money has been transferred to the wrong account, need a bribe to get it back ... the scammer needs money for a passport to get to South Africa so they can find out what has gone wrong.

Are you seeing a pattern here? I can personally guarantee one thing – you will never see the money; you will not even get the money back that you have given them.

Most people give up after they lose about fifteen to twenty thousand dollars. The highest I have ever heard of is one hundred and sixty thousand dollars – the victim had stolen so much money that he ended up going to prison for six years.

Chapter 35 - Winning the lottery

Winning the lottery seems to be a dream that most people have. Ask them what they would do with a lottery win and they can answer very quickly as they have day dreamed about it at some stage.

Playing the lottery is simple; you buy a ticket and see if it wins. Every so often I see new systems that guarantee that you can win the lottery; these systems cost money and have been proven not to work.
Think about it, if the system really did work then why would a person sell it? Why not just keep using the system in order to keep winning the lottery? If a system that worked was sold then there would be more winners and that would mean prizes would be of a smaller value.

The latest scam sweeping the Internet involves lotteries, and they usually originate from Europe.

This scam is simple and effective. People really get sucked in for this one because they don't believe that Europeans would run such a scam!
The belief that European lotteries are run by governments also leads people into a false sense of security. The problem is that scammers, not governments, run these so called 'lotteries'!

There are many scams that can be run from a lottery.
The first one is simple; the scammer gets you to pay for 'taxes' before the winnings can be released, this is illegal but victims seem to accept it. Every legal lottery in the world (that is taxed) will take the tax out of the winnings, and then transfer the remaining funds.
You simply need to pay the five thousand dollars in taxes to receive your nine hundred and fifty thousand dollar winnings.
Note that the bribe amount could be anything - five thousand is simply an example.

The other scam is if they get your personal information so they can then use it for illegal purposes. This is a type of 'identity fraud'.

Another method these scammers use to scam money is to convince you that you need to open a bank account with them and, to open this account, you must make a minimum deposit of funds.
To start with you send fifteen hundred dollars (this amount is an example, the scams that I have seen range from a thousand to three thousand dollars – fifteen being the most common), via a 'Western Union' wire transfer in order to open a bank account to which the winnings will be transferred. This money is actually pocketed by the scammers as there is no bank.

Example 1

contact the paying bank
Millions Lottery.

We are pleased to inform you of the result of Million Lottery, which was Held on the 1st , March 2007.Your e-mail address attached to ticket number:14-18-34-45-67 (76-32)With Prize Number (match 5):222000009 drew a prize of 2,000, 000.00 (two Million Euros). This lucky draw came first in the 2nd Category of the Sweepstake.You will receive the sum of 2,000,000.00 (two Million Euros) from our Authorized bank. Because of some mix-up with sweepstake prizes, including the time limited placed on the payment of your prize:€2,000, 000.00 euros, we advice that you keep all information about this prize confidential until your funds: 2,000,000.00 Euros will be transferred to you by our bank.You must adhere to this instruction, strictly, to avoid any delay with the release of your
funds to your person. This program has been abused severally in past, so we are doing our best to forestall further occurrence of false claims. This sweepstake was conducted under the watchful eyes of 8,000 spectators. Your e-mail address attached to e-ticket number 14-18-34-45-67 (76-32) was selected and; it came out first by an e-ballot draw from over 250,000 e-mail addresses (personal and corporate e-mail addresses). This program is sponsored by CFI to compensate faithful internet suffers around the globe.Congratulations for becoming one of the few lucky winners.With your permission, your e-mail will also be included in the next Sweepstake of 20Million Euros.You must claim our prize: 2,000,000.00 Euros not later than 7-days from the moment you receive this e-mail. In order to avoid unnecessary Delays with your claim from the bank; please contact them immediately,and quote your winning and personal information now,and in all your Correspondence with the Bank. Here is the contact

Information:Bank: Premuim Bank

Attention: Mr.Fred Van

Africanaplain 75, 1106 bJ, Amsterdam, Netherlands.
E-mail: laagstebank1nltd@aim.com
Phone:+31-614-998-371
Fax: + 31-84-757-1908

Furnish them with the following:
(i). Your name(s),
(ii) Your telephone and fax numbers
(iii) Your contact address.
(iv) Your winning information (including amount won).
(v)occupation and position in office
Congratulations in Advance!!!

Yours Faithfully,

Von Adrian (Ms.) CPA.
Coordinator: Millions Lottery .

COMMENT: If you do fill out the form and send it back you will have given the scammers all your personal details; this leads to identity fraud.

What makes me shake my head in disbelief is why I have to tell them my 'occupation and position in office'.

Is this draw really done under the eyes of 8,000 spectators? Where did all the spectators stand? Or was it over the Internet? If it was, then why couldn't everyone else get to see it? Wouldn't a free lottery get lots of media interest so there would be lots of interested spectators?

Example 2

RE: NOTIFICATION

Dear Winner

We apologise, for the delay of your payment and all the inconveniences and inflict that we might have indulged you through. However, we were having some minor problems with our payment system, which is inexplicable, and have held us stranded and indolent, not having the aspiration to devote our 100% assiduity in accrediting foreign payments.

We apologise once again, from the records of outstanding winners due for payment with {Euro African Lottery Award 2006}your name and particular was discovered as next on the list of the outstanding winners who have not yet received their payments. I wish to inform you now that the square peg is now in the square whole and can be voguished for that your payment is being processed and will be released to you as soon as you respond to this letter. Also note that from our record in our file, your outstanding winning payment is US$950,000.00 (Nine Hundred and Fifty Thousand, United States Dollars)

Payment will be made to you in a certified bank draft or wire transfer into a nominated bank account of your choice, as soon as you get in touche with our registered claim agent, MR.Chris Allen, E-mail: chrisallen_4@myway.com and provide him with the following details, as this will enable him to process and release of your cash prize without any delay.

1) Your full name, address.
2) Phone, fax.
3) Company name, position.
4) Profession, age and marital status.

Be informed that the appointed agent will be required to swear affidavits of lotto claim on your behalf. Upon reply to this mail, please reply through this email address: chrisallen_4@myway.com

Yours Sincerely,

Mr Ken Peter

92

Lottery Coordinator

COMMENT: Why do they need my marital status? Or age? Or profession? Because they need that information when filling out credit applications in your name that's why, it's identity theft and it's hell if you are the victim.

Example 3

Euromillion UK Lotto.
49/56 Featherstone Street
LONDON EC 1Y 8SY
GREAT BRITAIN

Ref. N°: UK/007/05/12/EU.
Batch. N°: GHT/2907/333/07.

YOUR E-MAIL ADDRESS WON THE LOTTERY.

We wish to congratulate you over your email success in our computer balloting sweepstake held on 24th March,2007. This is a millennium scientific computer game in which email addresses were used. It is a promotional program aimed at encouraging internet users; therefore you do not need to buy ticket to enter for it.

Your email address attached to ticket star number (4-5) drew the EUROMILLION lucky numbers 3-19-26-49-50 which consequently won The draw in the Second category.You have been approve for the star prize of Pounds 700,000.00. (Seven Hundred Thousand,Pounds sterling).

CONGRATULATIONS !!!

You are advised to keep this winning very confidential until you receive your lump prize in your account or optional cheque issuance to you. This is a protective measure to avoid double claiming by people you may tell as we have had cases like this before, please send your Full Name,Home and Office Tel & Fax Number, Mobile Tel Number and your winning ticket number,reference numbers and amount won information for processing of your winning fund to our registered claim agent in addrres below:
****
Euromillion Trust Security Service
Mr.Guido Mihan
Address: 49/56 Feather stone Street
United Kingdom
E-mail:verifyingdepartment2007@yahoo.co.uk

Phone:+447031848249 or+447024026795
****

Rememer, all winning must be claimed not later than 28th April, 2007. Please note, in order to avoid unnecessary delays and

complications, remember to quote your reference number and batch number in all correspondence.Furthermore, should there be any change of address do inform our agent as soon as possible.
Once again congratulations.
Best regard,
Mrs. Emily Simon,
Lottery coordinator.

The information transmitted is intended only for the person or entity to whom or which it is addressed. Unauthorised use, disclosure or copying is strictly prohibited. The sender accepts no liability for the improper transmission of this communication nor for any delay in its receipt
****

COMMENT: *'You are advised to keep your winnings very confidential...'* This is to stop you from telling someone who points out the obvious flaws in this scheme. Someone may have given you this book to read simply to point out that this is a scam.

Example 4

You won $250.000.00! Yahoo! Msn! Mail congratulates you!

THE YAHOO LOTTERY INTERNATIONAL. INC

YAHOO LOTTERY INTL INC
Barley House Harold Road
Sutton, Greater London Sm1 4te
United Kingdom.

Attention: Lottery Winner,

YAHOO LOTTERY WINNING NOTIFICATION

We happily announce to you the draw of the Yahoo Lottery Intl Inc programs held on the 28th of February 2007 in London. Your e-mail address attached to ticket number: 56475600545 188 with Serial number 5388/02 drew the lucky numbers: 31-6-2613357, which subsequently won you the lottery in the 2nd category. You are therefore, been approved to claim a total sum of TWO HUNDRED AND FIFTY THOUSAND US DOLLARS ($250,000) for the 28th of February 2007 lottery win promotion which is organized by MSN & YAHOO LOTTORY INTL INC .Every month.

YAHOO, collects all the E MAIL I D of the people that subscribes to yahoomail, msn, hotmail, aol, altavista, and others online, among the billions that subscribe to us only five people will be merge for winnings we only select five people every Month as our winners through electronic balloting System without the winner applying, we are congratulating you for having been one of the lucky people that won for this month..

PAYMENT OF PRIZE AND CLAIM

you are to contact your Claims Agent on or before your date of Claim, Winners shall be paid in accordance with his/her Settlement Centre.

Yahoo Lottery Prize must be claimed no later than 15 days from date of Draw Notification after the Draw date in which Prize has won. Any prize not claimed within this period will be forfeited and retrieved

These are your identification numbers....

Yahoo! Lottery Results:
Batch number....................Lwh 09102
Lotto number.......................Lwh35447
Winning number..................Lwh09788

These numbers are your winning identification numbers, that you will
send to your claims agent,send identification and details of claim to.

Mr. Patrick . C. Gill
Email:globalhandsinc@netscape.net
Tel:+445600011543 +447031947171
Fax:+448704900678 :+44712475425

You are therefore advise to quote the following information to
the Clams Agent to facilitate them to process the transfer of your fund without delay.

Serial number 5388/02
Draw lucky numbers: 31-6-2613357
Ticket number: 56475600545 188
Batch number....................Lwh 09102
Lotto number.......................Lwh35447
Winning number..................Lwh09788

Your winning fall in Africa-Asia! This promotion takes place every Month .Please note that your lucky winning number falls
within our European booklet representative office in Africa-Asia as indicated in your play coupon.In view of this, your TWO
HUNDRED AND FIFTY THOUSAND US DOLLARS ($250,000) would be released to you by any of our payment offices in
Africa-Asia.Our agent zoned for Africa paying bank will immediately commence the process to facilitate the release of your
funds as soon as you contact him.

NOTE: YOU ARE STRONGLY ADVISED TO KEEP ALL YOUR WINNING CONFIDENTIAL TILL CLAIM IS MADE TO
AVOID WRONG CLAIMING.ANY BREACH OF CONFIDENCIAL DISQULIFIES YOU FROM GETTING YOUR PRIZE.

Mrs.Darryn Clarke
Online coordinator Yahoo
International Lottery Program. .
ATTN: ONCE AGAIN WE THE ENTIRE STAFF OF THE YAHOO INTERNATIONAL LOTTERY WE ARE
CONGRATULATING YOU FOR YOUR WINNINGS, SO IN ORDER FOR US TO PROCESS YOUR WINNINGS, YOU
ARE TO FILL AND RETURN THE VERIFICATION AND CLEARANCE FORM BELOW TO YOUR CLAIMS AGENT
THROUGH THIS EMAIL OR FAX BELOW:

OSA CLAIMS PROCESSING LOTTERY AGENT
Contact Person: Mr. Patrick. C. Gill
Email: globalhandsinc@netscape.net
Tel:+44 70111 47935 44702 409 7893
Fax:+44870 479 3935 +44870 479 3999

..
CONGRATULATIONS ONCE AGAIN.

VERIFICATION AND CLERANCE FORM
1. FULL NAMES:_____(BENEFICIARY NAME)
2. RESIDENTIAL ADDRESS:_____
3. SEX:_____
4. DATE AND PLACE OF BIRTH::_____
5. MARITAL STATUS:_____
6. OCCUPATION:_____
7. E-MAIL ADDRESS:_____
8. TELEPHONE NUMBER:_____
9. FAX NUMBER::_____
A. BATCH NUMBER:_____SERIALNO:_____

95

B. TICKET NUMBER:_____ WINNING NO:_____
10. BRIEF DESCRIPTION OF COMPANY/INDIVIDUAL_____
11. AMOUNT WON:_____
12. COUNTRY OF RESIDENCE:_____
13. NEXT OF KIN NAME AND ADDRESS:_____
14:DATE NOTIFIED _____
15:PASSPORT NO:_____

PLEASE NOTE: You must have to attach a scanned copy of your international passport, Driver's licence. Is mandatory

DECLARATION:
I...HEREBY DECLARE THAT THE ABOVE DATA ARE TRUE. IN CASE OF ANY UNFORSEEN CIRCUSTANCE, MY NEXT OF KIN HAS THE RIGHT TO CLAIM MY TOTAL WINNINGS. (OVERSEAS SUBCRIBERS AGENT) SHALL ACT AS MY AGENT IN FACILITATING THE TRANSFER OF THE TOTAL FUND TO ME.
DATE:
YOUR FULL NAMES:

Upon receipt of the duly requested data, Our agent will proceed for proper verification and furnish you with the contact information of the payment Bank in the region where your winning numbers fall within so you can proceed with effecting the release of your claim in anyway you deem fit.

The Yahoo.com staff
Yahoo.com http://www.yahoo.com

COMMENT: Note all the personal information that is required? Why do I have to scan a copy of my passport to send them? This is definitely an identity theft scam.

Another logical question – why aren't the lottery numbers that are assigned to email addresses actually sent to those people before the lottery? Wouldn't that make people more excited to know that they are in a lottery?

I have also been informed that the telephone number starting with '+44 70' is a redirection number; this phone call could be redirected to anywhere in the world.

Example 5

NEDERLAND DAYZERS:
PALEISSTRAAT 5, 2514 JA,
THE HAGUE, THE NETHERLANDS.
Official Website: www.dayzers.nl,

RESULT MONTH OF FEBRUARY PROGRAM:

These are your winning information's:
TICKET NUMBER: DZNL 492 - 714 - 027 / 2006
LUCKY NUMBER: 09, 22, 36, 61, 63, 79, 84
REFRENCE NUMBER: NUWL / DZNL / 48326MST
BATCH NUMBER: DTOW 1396 62U7A

OUR DEAR WINNER,

96

YOU WON THE SUM OF (ONE MILLION EURO) FROM DAYZERS LOTTERY AND GAMING CORPORATION. THE WINNING TICKET WAS SELECTED FROM A DATA BASE OF INTERNET E-MAIL USERS, FROM WHICH YOUR E-MAIL ADDRESS CAME OUT AS THE WINNING COUPON.

WE THEREBY CONTACT YOU TO CLAIM YOUR WINNING AMOUNT QUICKLY AS THIS IS A MONTHLY LOTTERY. FAILURE TO CLAIM YOUR WIN WILL RESULT INTO THE REVERSION OF THE WINNING SUM TO OUR FOLLOWING MONTH LOTTERY. (CLAIMS DEADLINE, 31ST OF MARCH, 2007). PLEASE CONTACT OUR APPROVED CLAIM DEPARTMENT FOR YOUR REGION WITH YOUR WINNING NUMBER.
BE INFORMED, DUE TO THE MIXUP OF CERTAIN NAMES,YOU ARE ADVISED TO KEEP YOUR WINNING INFORMATION CONFIDENTIAL UNTIL YOUR CLAIM HAS BEEN PROCESSED AND YOUR MONEY PAID TO YOU.

DAYZERS ONLINE LOTTERY.
DR. JOHAN GALLAGHER.
DAYZERS CLAIMS DEPARTMENT.
TEL: +31-620-889-086
E-MAIL: dyzdpt@aim.com, dyzdpt@netscape.net

REGARDS,
MRS. MAUREEN VAN HOUDT.
DIRECTOR OF DAYZERS LOTTERY ONLINE.

Example 6

While I was writing this book my son received one of the best scam emails that I had seen in a long time; this was received via his Yahoo email account (which has no spam filter).

MICROSOFT WINDOWS GLOBAL E-MAIL LOTTERY
INTERNATIONAL PRIZE AWARD DEPARMENT
HEREENSTRAAT 212 1012KK
AMSTERDAM NETHERLANDS.

OFFICIAL WINNING NOTIFICATION

DEAR WINNER:

It is obvious that this notification will come to you as a suprise but please read it carefully as we congratulate you over your success in the following official publication of results of the E-mail electronic online Sweepstakes organized by Microsoft, in conjunction with the foundation for the promotion of software products, (F.P.S.), held on the 23rd of April2007, in Amsterdam The Netherlands.

Wherein your electronic email address emerged as one of the online
winning emails in the 3rd category and therefore attracted a cash award of 470,000.00Euros(Four hundred and seventy thousand Euros only).

Our winners are arranged into four categories with different winning prizes accordingly in each category. They are arranged in this format below:

CATEGORY	NO. OF WINNERS		WINNING PRIZES
1st.	2	1,000,000.00euros each	
2ND.	8	750,000.00euros each	
3rd.	13	470,000.00euros each	
4TH. each	27		170,000.00euros

We write to officially notify you of this award and to advise you to contact the processing office immediately upon receipt of this message for more information concerning the verification, processing and eventual payment of the above prize to you.

It is important to note that your award information was released with the following particulars attached to it.

Microsoft Winning Numbers						
Award Numbers:	NL	5	6	7	7	6	5
Email Ticket Numbers:	NL	5	5	5	2	6	96
Batch Numbers:	MC	11	8	3	4	5	PDH/EU
File Reference Number:	HL	55	64	06	0	7	MIC'S
Serial Numbers	McST	0	0	7	NL	46	57

For verification purpose be sure to include:
(1) mailing address.
(2) Tel/Fax numbers.
(3) Nationality/Country.
(4) Full Names
(5) Microsoft winning numbers

Please contact your Validating Officer for VALIDATION of your winning within Twenty-nine working days of this winning notification. Winnings that are not validated within Twenty-nine working days of winning notification are termed void and invalid. You are required to mention the above particulars of your award in every correspondence to enable the Agent validate your winning.

****

PROCESSING OFFICER (Mr Mark Roberts)
MICROSOFT CLAIMS OFFICE(NL)
TEL:+31-614-997-584
FAX:+31-847-259-825
E-mail: processingoffice0@searchmachine.com
****

The Microsoft Internet E-mail lottery Awards is sponsored by our CEO/Chairman and consortium of software promotion companies. The Intel Group, Toshiba, Dell Computers and other International Companies. The Microsoft Internet E-mail draw is held periodically and is organized to encourage the use of the Internet and promote computer literacy worldwide.

CONGRATULATIONS! Once again on behalf of all our staff.

Yours faithfully,
CHRISTINE TURKER (Mrs)
MICROSOFT E-MAIL LOTTERY PROMOTION COORDINATOR.

COMMENT: Whoever created this put a lot of time and effort into it. The spelling and grammar are correct; graphics are correct and displayed professionally.
But, again, this is totally FALSE – there is no lottery.

Example 7

No more email examples as I'm sure the previous six have shown you what to look out for.

I just thought I would finish this chapter with a graphic that appeared on one of the spam emails.

You DON'T need to be a Yahoo Member?? If this lottery was real don't you think that Yahoo would only allow Yahoo registered members to be in it so they could get more members?

Wouldn't Yahoo advertise that they run a lottery in the first place so they can sign up more members?

Chapter 36 - Internet Viruses

Every birthday I receive a virtual birthday card from friends. An email arrives saying that I have a 'virtual greeting card' waiting for me to download and view.

The key factor you need to know is that a greeting card will always show you who it is being sent to and who sent it.

So far 'scammers' have run all the scams in this book; Internet viruses are different as 'hackers' control them.
Hackers try to take control of your computer for a variety of reasons, these include (but not limited too) –
- Recording your keyboard strokes; this will give them all your passwords without your knowledge.
- Allowing them to send out their spam email from your computer; this way you get the blame for sending out the spam.
- Storing Child pornography on your computer; this way the hackers don't get caught with the offending material, you do.
- Using your computer to launch 'attacks' on other computers.
- Delete parts of your hard drive. Hackers do this for fun (like others would play sport for fun), so deleting your hard drive is 'fun' for them.

All of this is done without your knowledge. This is why you MUST have a firewall on your computer; and don't forget to keep it updated!

This chapter will concentrate on the Greeting card virus but that is certainly not the only method that a hacker uses to try to gain control of your computer.

Simple Viruses

Before we start on the greeting card virus I will point out several methods that hackers use to spread viruses.

A virus can only get onto a computer by being installed; to do this the user must run the program (it can't install itself). The catch here is to try and trick the user into running the program as it is highly unlikely that a user would knowingly install a virus.

The easiest way is for the hacker to send an email to a victim with a video attached called 'Paris Hilton Video', the victim clicks on the video in order to view it but nothing happens

– no video starts! What has happened is that there was no video, instead a virus has been installed on the computer. Notice that the victim has clicked on the email to run the virus program, even though they thought they were going to be watching a video.

I know this one from personal experience as I was working at an office where the boss opened this virus. The first thing a virus will do is use the email program on the host computer to send a copy of itself to everyone that is in the 'friends' file; this means it will send a copy of itself to everyone that the host computer knows.
In this instance that meant all the workers got a copy of the virus! As I was the computer I.T person for the office I was the first to receive it so I could forewarn every one else so they could delete it straight away.
The funny part here was that everyone in the office now knew that the boss had attempted to open the 'Paris Hilton video'.

Emails that have attachments that end with '.exe' are usually viruses. Examples include 'happy.exe', 'openme.exe', 'lovelife.exe'. There are thousands of viruses floating around the Internet at any one time with hundreds of different names.
The first thing that nearly all viruses try to do first is to send themselves onto other computers; so if you get an email from a friend don't automatically assume that it is legitimate.
An email from a 'friend' will tell you that this 'program' (the virus) will show you how much they like you; if it's a virus then your friend didn't know about it so don't take it personally! (Unless they really do hate you!)

Greeting Card Virus

So lets get to the main part of this chapter, tricky greeting cards!

The objective of this scam is to get you to click on the link in the email; this will take you to a web site that asks you to download a program in order to view the card.

DON'T.

There is no card and the program is a computer virus.

Just by visiting a web site doesn't mean a virus is downloaded onto your computer system, you need to actually run the program for the virus to work.

Example 1

Hello, you just received an electronic greeting from a friend !

To view your eCard, please click on the following link :

http://www.bluemountain.com/view.pd?i=164213761&~~~2435&~~~&source=bma999
(Your postcard will be available for 60 days http://bluemountains.kokocards.com/main.php

If you have any comments or questions, please visit http://www.bluemountain.com/customer/emailus.pd?source=bma999

Thanks for using BlueMountain.com.

COMMENT:

When a person sends a greeting card they are asked for their own name and the name of the person that they are sending them too.

First thing that is wrong is that it DOESN'T say whom the greeting card is for. A legitimate one will say 'Hello James,' while this one simply says 'Hello'.

Next problem is that it doesn't say who sent it; a legitimate one will say 'you have received an electronic greeting from Katie', not 'a friend'.

I know I've explained this several times in this book but I'm going to explain it again - if you hold the mouse pointer over the link in the email, without clicking on it, then the real web address will appear.

'Blue Mountain' is a real virtual company with real virtual greeting cards, unfortunately their name is being used for illegal purposes. "www.bluemountain.com" is the real web site but as you can see in the circle the link actually leads to "bluemountain.kokcards.com" which is a fake web site.

Example 2

Hi, someone has sent you a greeting card!
Please click the link below to view your Greeting
Card....If the link is not clickable just copy and
paste or type the address in your browser..ENJOY!!
this is a flash executable that you can save on your hard drive so you can look at it anytime you would like!

Your Greeting Card http://www.2000Greetings.com/pickup.htm?prd=111970425U8H0

http://www.2000greetings.us.to/a_friend.exe

If you have trouble using the link we provided, please follow these steps:

1. Click this link to go to our homepage,
or copy and paste it into your browser's address line:http://www.2000Greetings.com

2. Enter your card ID 111970425U8H0 in the Pick up ID Box
Your card will be available for 20 days. If you'd like to send a card yourself please go to :http://www.2000Greetings.com

Get your 2000Greetings.com Reminder Service
and Printable Calendars http://www.2000Greetings.com/reminder

COMMENT: *2000greetings* is another legitimate company that has been tarnished by hackers.

Click on this link and you will automatically be downloading the virus!
Notice in the real web address (circled) that you will be going to the web site of 'www.2000greetings.us.to', this is a fake web site. The last part of the web address, 'a_friend.exe', is the name of the actual virus that will be downloaded if you click on this link.
Items that end in '.exe' are programs. As a side note '.exe' stand for 'executable'.

The only '.exe' files that you should run are legal copies of software that you have bought from a store, or downloaded from a reputable site on the Internet. Don't run any programs if you don't know where they originated.

Example 3

You have just received a virtual postcard from a family member!

You can pick up your postcard at the following web address:

http://www2.postcards.org/?a91-valets-cloud-31337

http://203.28.113.6/~air-stream/postcard.exe

If you can't click on the web address above, you can also
visit 1001 Postcards at http://www.postcards.org/postcards/
and enter your pickup code, which is: a91-valets-cloud-mad

(Your postcard will be available for 60 days.)

Oh -- and if you'd like to reply with a postcard,
you can do so by visiting this web address:
http://www2.postcards.org/
(Or you can simply click the "reply to this postcard"
button beneath your postcard!)

We hope you enjoy your postcard, and if you do,
please take a moment to send a few yourself!

Regards,
1001 Postcards
http://www.postcards.org/postcards/

COMMENT: Again, this links directly to the virus ("postcard.exe"). Again, it tells me that the postcard was sent to me by a family member but fails to mention whom.

Example 4

> ### Hello friend !
> **You have just received a postcard Greeting from someone who cares about you !**
>
> This is a part of the message:
> "Hy there! It has been a long time since I haven't heared about you!
> I've just found out about this service from Amy, a friend of mine who also told me that ..."
>
> If you'd like to see the rest of the message click **here to receive your animated** Greeting !
>
> http://ns2.netcon.nl/gift.jpg.exe
>
> Thank you for using www.postcard.com services !!!
> Please take this opportunity to let your friends hear about us by sending them a postcard from our collection !

COMMENT: Same scam as all the others but one extra point needs to be made.

If a filename ends in '.exe' then it is an 'executable' (program) and needs to be run. If it ends in '.mpeg' then it is a movie, '.jpg' is a photo and '.mp3' means a song. These are the four main ones but there are hundreds of others.

What this means is that if a friend sends you a file that ends in '.jpg' (note that '.jpeg' is the same as '.jpg') then you know it's a picture so you can open it without the fear of it being a virus.

What the above example is trying to do is trick you into believing it is a picture by calling the file 'gift.jpg.exe' – only the LAST letters count after the LAST dot, so this is an '.exe'.

Side note –
- MPEG stands for 'Motion Picture Experts group' - Movies.
- JPG (or JPEG) stands for 'Joint Photographic Experts Group' - Pictures.
- Mp3 stands for 'MPEG-1 Audio Layer-3' - Songs.

Example 5

```
From: aol com
Date: 18/02/2007 02:05:49 PM
To: ███████████████████
Subject: Please Update Your Account!




You have received a postcard from a family member!



You can pick up your postcard at the following web address:
```

COMMENT: This one was a bit of a botch up. Hackers and scammers run hundreds of scams at the same time (it's a full time job for them) and in this instance they have accidentally combined two scams in the one email.

In the 'from:' section it is from aol.com and the subject is 'Please update your account'; this is part of a scam directed towards AOL users to trick them into handing over their account details.
The body of the email is the Greeting card virus scam.

Chapter 37 - Affiliate programs

Affiliate programs are great for earning a bit of money on the side if you have a successful web site.

If you are running google ads on your web site then you are running an affiliate program of sorts. I run several affiliate programs from my web site so I can vouch that this is a good way to make some extra money.

I have never come across a scam affiliate program (I'm sure there are ones) but in this chapter I think I should point out the potential pitfalls of being in a legitimate program. Note that I will only point out the scams in BEING an associate, not setting up an associate system.

If you are an affiliate then you will have been given an *affiliate ID* which is used by the system to work out who gets paid what.

Scammers have worked out how to infiltrate unsecured web sites and CHANGE the 'affiliate ID' to their own. If this trick is done quietly and discreetly then it could be months before the affiliate (you) realises what has been done, and even though it is quite easy to change the affiliate ID back to your own you would have lost months of revenue in the meantime.

You will not be able to get any lost revenue back from the affiliation program even if it is proven that you have been scammed; it is too much trouble for the affiliate to try to work out who is owed what.

If an affiliate program does allow 'charge backs' then it can lead to false accusations; scammers might accuse YOU of doing it to their web site and that you are the thief, that causes all sorts of headaches for the affiliate program.

Remember the golden rule – scammers will do anything to make money and they don't care who suffers.

Summary

Hopefully after reading this book you will have learnt how to spot a spam email. Here I will repeat the main lessons –

- If the email seems suspicious then it most probably is.
- If you can't work out if an email is legitimate or not then send it to me at james@thebestscams.com and I'll tell you.
- Never click on a link in an email.
- When in an email, if you hold your mouse pointer over a web link and DON'T click on it then the real destination web address will appear.
- Taxes, and bank fees, are taken out of winnings and money transfers before they are transferred; you NEVER have to pay any money up front if a transaction is legitimate.
- If an email defies logic then don't believe it; scammers need you to suspend reality in order to believe the scam. The more money that can be made, the more willing victims are to defy logic.
- Any problems with your account will show up on the web site; so if an email tells you that there are problems then go to the web site directly, don't automatically assume that the email is correct. If the web site doesn't show a problem then the email is fake.
- I receive thousands of scam emails each year; it's a business for scammers so don't take it personally.
- Never reply to a scam (or spam) email, it only encourages them.

STOP PRESS

I've spent over a year writing this book and I'm currently on my sixth (and hopefully last) re-write.

Today I have received a scam email that has defied one of the key points I have tried to make in this book -

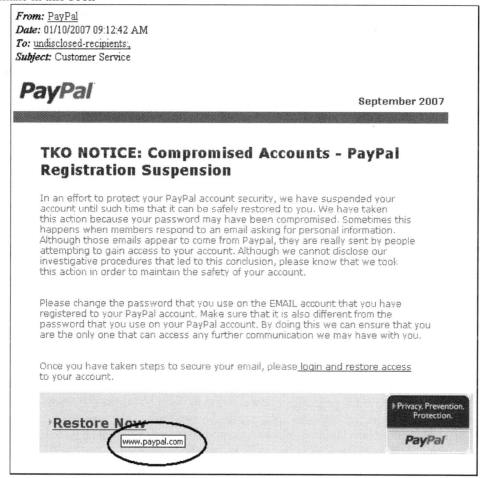

All book I have tried to teach the message that if you place the mouse pointer over the link then the real web address will appear. I have placed a black circle around the web address that is displayed – and it's 'www.paypal.com'! This email is still a fraud though.

Click on this link though and you will be taken to the following web site.

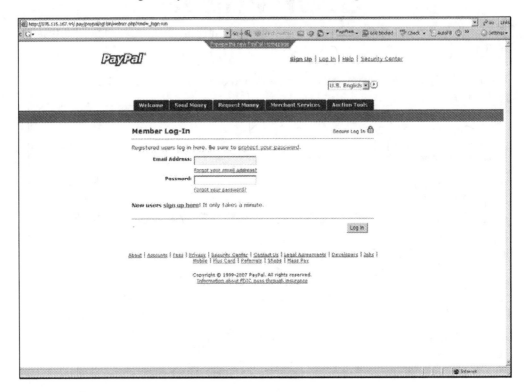

Mistakes made (and there weren't many) –

- On the email it has been sent to 'undisclosed recipients'; the email is dated 'September 2007' while the email was actually sent on the first of October.
- If I check the properties of the email it has been sent from the email address of 'intel@aol.com'.
- The web site address does not start with 'https://www.paypal.com'.
- In the middle of the page it states 'Secure log in' with the padlock symbol – this is not correct, the padlock must appear at the bottom right of the page. This page has been displayed in 'Internet Explorer', other programs display the padlock in different parts of the page but never in the middle.

REMEMBER – Don't click on an email, type 'www.paypal.com' into the address bar of your web browser.

www.ingramcontent.com/pod-product-compliance
Lightning Source LLC
LaVergne TN
LVHW080101070326
832902LV00014B/2347